DEATH OF THE MIDDLE CLASS + SECULAR ECONOMIC STAGNATION = HOW TRADE WITH COMMUNIST CHINA IS DESTROYING DEMOCRACY & CAPITALISM

HOW LIBERAL ECONOMIC THEORY HAS BEEN MISREPRESENTED TO JUSTIFY TRADE WITH A COMMUNIST COUNTRY, AND HOW TO SAVE OUR WAY OF LIFE BEFORE IT GOES THE WAY OF THE SOVIET UNION

MARK JEIA

authorHOUSE®

AuthorHouse™ UK
1663 Liberty Drive
Bloomington, IN 47403 USA
www.authorhouse.co.uk
Phone: 0800.197.4150

Published by AuthorHouse 01/26/2017

ISBN: 978-1-5246-7678-0 (sc)
ISBN: 978-1-5246-7679-7 (hc)
ISBN: 978-1-5246-7680-3 (e)

Print information available on the last page.

This book is printed on acid-free paper.

Table of Contents

"Truth exists, only lies have to be invented"

L.M. Montgomery

INTRODUCTION – THE PROBLEM

The decline of living standards in developed countries – is the global capitalist economy going the way of the Soviet Union?

Unfortunately, it is increasingly obvious for everyone living in the developed world, and even most of the developing world, that over the past 20-25 years, the economic and political system has broken down in terms of its ability to deliver a decent, middle-class level of living standards for the majority of our population.

From Manchester to Malaga, Tampa to Chicago, Calgary to Tokyo, we see a sad but clear common thread: the disappearance of medium-skilled, decent-paying jobs, especially in manufacturing, which have historically provided the base for the middle class. Auto workers, steel workers, and many others we can think of.

We can also see the results – the growing threat to the pillars of our entire economic and political system including democracy, freedom of speech, respect for diversity, and many other things that we take for granted today but which our grandparents certainly didn't take for granted in their times.

If you have not been living under a rock in Manhattan, it should be obvious to you too.

There is a clear trend of declining opportunities for the younger generations. Most of all, we are witnessing the slow death of the hope for a better future, and the hope for a world in which each generation would have higher living standards than their parents – a world in which the fruits of innovation would be enjoyed by all, not because of some kind of state intervention or charitable action towards income redistribution, but just because capitalism was set up in such a way as to make this process automatic and indeed inevitable.

While I studied economics, I am not a big fan of using statistics to elaborate the obvious. But just to show this growing sense of stagnation and indeed decline is a generalized problem, consider this:

FIGURE 1 – REAL MEDIAN HOUSEHOLD INCOME IN THE USA, 1999-2013

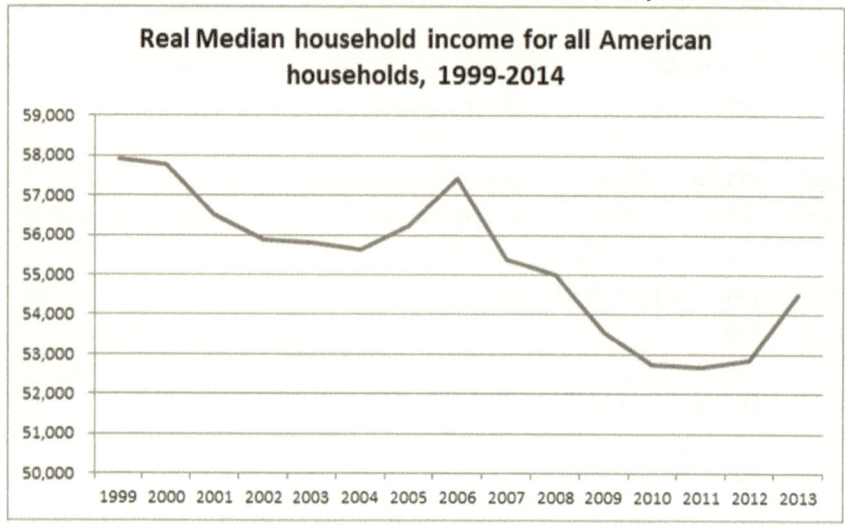

(Source: Author, US Census data)

FIGURE 2 – REAL MEDIAN HOUSEHOLD INCOME IN THE USA SINCE 1950

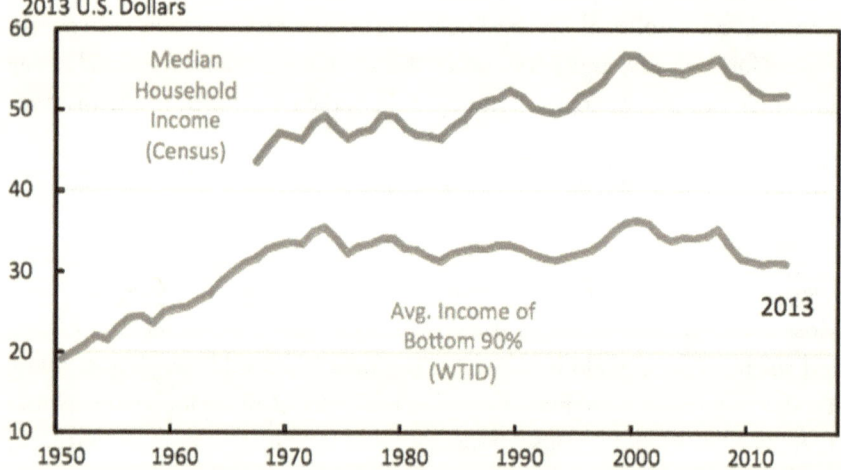

(Source; Council of Economic Advisers – 2015 Report to the President https://www.whitehouse.gov/administration/eop/cea/economic-report-of-the-President/2015)

FIGURE 3 – REAL AVERAGE INCOME FOR THE BOTTOM 90% IN JAPAN, GERMANY, ITALY, UK, FRANCE, CANADA AND THE USA, 1950-2013.

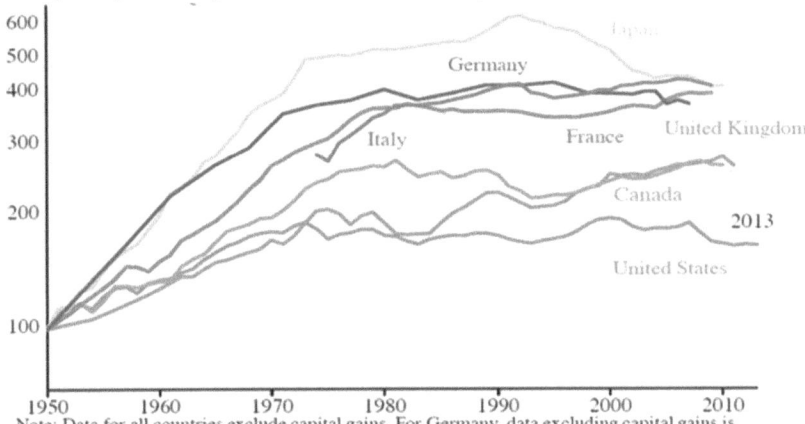

Note: Data for all countries exclude capital gains. For Germany, data excluding capital gains is unavailable after 1998, so this chart displays data including capital gains adjusted for the historical relationship between capital-inclusive and capital-exclusive incomes. Italian data begins in 1974 and is indexed to the average of the other series at that point. Italian data is calculated by CEA from the income level and share of the top 10 percent as provided by the World Top Incomes Database. Source: World Top Incomes Database; Saez (2015); CEA calculations.

(Source: Council of Economic Advisers – 2015 Report to the President https://www. whitehouse.gov/administration/eop/cea/economic-report-of-the-President/2015)

All the data that we have points into the same direction. In pretty much all major developed countries, we saw a stagnation or decline of standards of living over the past 20 years. Some countries did slightly better than others. But once we take a step back, we can see that there is a strong common trend across the entire group.

Having said that, I am not such a big fan of throwing statistics at people to substitute for a valid logical argument. In fact, I do not believe that any economic theory that is not derived from self-evident facts is defensible. Fortunately, almost all of them are. In economics, conclusions are often counterintuitively in the land of the fudge – economists will be the first to tell you that.

And just a note on median. It is very different than what is usually called the average, or mean. If you put a billionaire like Bill Gates in a room with 10 other people living on minimum wage, the average income (the sum of the income of all 11 people divided by the number of people in the room) will be very high. However, if you arrange all 11 from poorest to richest, the median income is the guy in the middle. In this case, it is the sixth richest guy. The median income of this room is therefore minimum wage. So median and other similar metrics are the key relevant measure to evaluate how standards of living have evolved over time. Using an average, in this sense, can therefore be very misleading.

The political, economic and academic establishment that currently rules the US, Europe and Japan has, in the past two decades, gone from denial that a general problem was taking place, to self-reassurances that it was temporary and reversible, and finally to a mix of confusion, desperation and wild goose-chasing. Like headless chickens, they have run all over the place with explanations and solutions. The "solutions" found were sometimes slightly helpful, sometimes harmful, but in all cases distractions from the true, increasingly obvious problem – the proverbial "elephant in the room", which people were and are still trying to ignore.

Everything from ultra-low interest rates to government spending, bank mergers, renewable energy incentives, artificially increasing the number of university graduates, and more, have been tried. At the same time, well-intentioned but misguided academics have blamed everything on ageing populations (demographic decline), lack of immigration, income inequality, the decline of labour unions, and comically either technological innovation being either too fast (for some) or too slow (for others).

They haven't tried animal sacrifices or self-flagellation yet, but considering their lack of attachment to reality, I would not put it past them. Recently, some central banks have tried printing money and what are known as negative interest rates, which means a saver is penalized for saving and a borrower gets paid to borrow.

I am sure we can all come up with many examples of the absurdity of the times we currently live in.

I work in global financial markets – what is called "Wall Street" in the US. I have watched daily and with increasing worry the tragedy of a system that has tried to look at everything but the "elephant" for a solution. What really worries me is that I am increasingly convinced that I have seen only one other such example of such a concerted attempt to ignore the obvious in the face of an increasingly desperate situation.

In only one other period in living memory did the elites of a system, blinded by a fanatical and unrealistic ideology, try to ignore for as long as possible the increasingly loud signals that the train was heading for the abyss.

That was the Soviet Union.

Figure 4 – GDP per capita – Soviet Union vs US

(Source: The Maddison-Project, http://www.ggdc.net/maddison/maddison-project/home.htm, 2013 version)

Just like our societies of today, the Soviet Union went from a period of incredible growth and optimism about the future, in which they had "won" the race for the future and "had history on their side", to a long period of stagnation and then decline in the standards of living for the average person.

This led to a period of internal conflict and self-doubt, very similar to what we have today, on to a general rejection of the entire establishment and finally a chaotic disintegration of the economic and political system. This process was gradual and almost imperceptible at first, but as it gathered speed it finally became a giant freight train that no one, inside or outside the country, could stop.

In the case of the Soviets, this was ultimately good. It was an inefficient, brutal system, which was ultimately based on ideologies that were the very opposite of human nature. However, it would not be so good to see the same thing happen in our societies.

If you look around, we can see growing signs that our system is similarly straining at the seams. This is evident in the rise of extremist political parties and political polarization more generally, racial and religious segregation, and the loss of faith of the general population in the institutions of the state and the political system more generally. The recent Brexit vote in the UK, with the country now set to leave the EU, is just one more example of the general unhappiness with the current system being manifested in unpredictable ways.

Ideology blinds you to the obvious truth, and the false economic "liberals" of today are pushing an ideology almost as far from real capitalism as the old Soviet ideology was.

Now, you may ask, aren't our current economic and political systems supposed to be the ultimate version of efficiency, the logical prosperity creation machine, the well-oiled Ferrari to the old, slow ZiL of the USSR? This is certainly how it has been sold to us, isn't it? "You may not like it but it's inevitable." "Some people will initially be impacted but in the end we will all end up in a prosperous paradise."

That's certainly how they have tried to sell it. There is only one ugly truth.

What we have today is almost as far from how a capitalist economy is supposed to work as the old Soviet system was, grey suits and funny accents aside. What we have today is a system that misrepresents the scripted speech of free markets, competition, meritocracy, fair compensation and checks/balances as a subterfuge to justify the pursuit of an increasingly unrealistic ideology that, I repeat, is counter to the very idea of capitalism, and indeed a growing threat to the continued functioning of the global capitalist economy.

This is because what is being sold as "liberal economic policies" to us today is almost "Soviet-like" in its negation of the basic law of economics, just like old communism was.

This law is the law of supply and demand.

When you have more lemons and less apples than what people normally want, apples are more expensive than lemons. Prices adjust to the relative balance of supply (what we have available) and what we demand. This is the fundamental logical pillar on which all economic theory is, or should have been, built upon. It is the essence of capitalism.

Who are these false economic "liberals"? I see no upside to finger pointing and name calling, but we should all know who they are. Those are the economists, politicians and journalists that have generally dominated policymaking over the past 20 years, and have misrepresented the true liberal economic theory to show the opposite of what it truly stands for.

These people have advanced the idea that free trade and heavy immigration flows with lower wage countries are a sure way to raise standards of living in developed countries. And they have also advanced the idea that open trade with a large communist country can be beneficial. Which is the opposite of what the essential laws of economics, based on market forces and supply and demand balance, have established over the years.

They often call themselves "free market" liberals, despite being proponents of the opposite of what free market and liberalism stands for.

The same kind of massive wealth destruction caused by the Communist system, which brought down the Soviet Union, is now also bringing down the global economy, as a result of free trade with Communist China.

Western democracy going the same way as the Soviet Union is not just a distant analogy. It holds a direct similarity caused by the *same* underlying economic factors.

The arbitrary inefficiency of communism killed the Soviet Union. The idea of a centrally planned economy, where what is produced, invested and consumed is decided by a bunch of government bureaucrats inside a dark room, instead of the more natural interaction between consumers and producers. Think of the movie "Moscow on the Hudson" - the long lines for products that everyone needs but they didn't have enough of, like shoes and toilet paper, and how even finding the right shoe size was a daily challenge.

And the arbitrary inefficiency of communism is killing western democracies. As the Chinese economy grows, bearing in mind that it is already a dominant player in the current global trading system, it spreads the impact of its own communist-oriented policies – bridges to nowhere, ghost cities, massive industrial overcapacity – to the rest of us. Because if they build a bridge or a steel plant that generates no economic value, the necessary inputs for that goes up in price, and that makes a bridge and everything that uses the same raw materials as steel less affordable to everyone else in the world. In an open global economy, what a communist state does affects everyone else, and generally waste resources for the global economic system as a whole.

Sorry, come again? Communism? Today? I thought it had been dead and buried since the late 1980s?

However, as we all know, the entire global economy has been heavily impacted by the communist, arbitrary decisions of the most important economic actor of the past 15-20 years!

The Communist Party of China! This organisation maintains a very strong grip on China's entire economy and society.

The presence of a large communist country such as China in the global trading system effectively changes the way the entire system works.

FIGURE 5 – CHINA SHARE OF GLOBAL DEMAND FOR KEY COMMODITIES

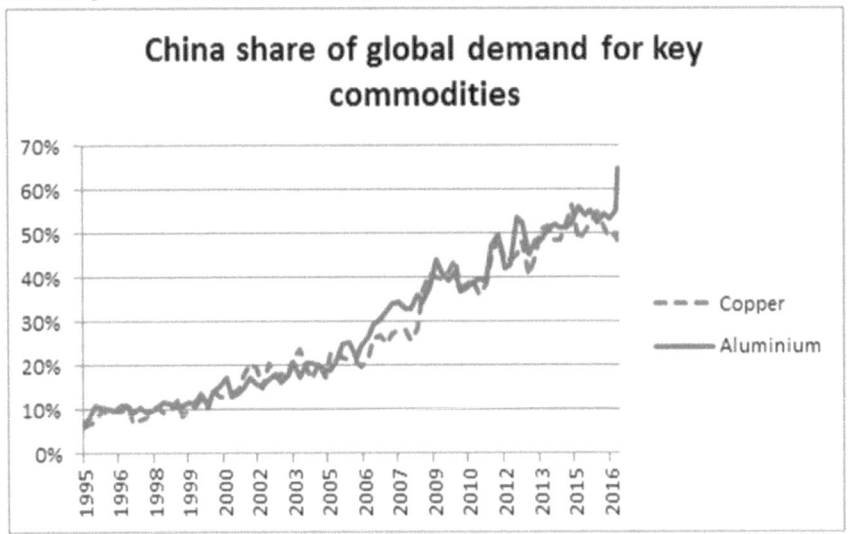

(Source: Author, elaboration of Bloomberg data)

While for some reason (in fact, for many reasons) mainstream media don't like to talk about it, most of China's political and economic system works almost exactly like that of the Soviet Union. Most of the key investment decisions of China are still state-mandated. The formal and informal structures that bind together both the public and the private sector of China are very similar to that of the Soviet Union.

However, when Soviet bureaucrats made stupid wealth-destroying decisions – like building bridges that no one needed, spending huge sums on the military, or pumping most of their money into "war supporting sectors" such as steel and mining as opposed to consumer goods (the similarities with Chinese policies over the past 20 years are striking) – the only parties to suffer were the people within the communist bloc. This is because the Soviet Union had very few links with the capitalist system. Those on the other side of the fence could therefore still enjoy a happy and prosperous life and patiently wait for the other side to crumble under the weight of their own problems.

Today, however, when the Chinese Communist Party makes stupid decisions – exactly like those described above – it impacts the entire global economy. If it decides to build a bridge to nowhere, raw materials become too expensive for your local government to repair your local bridge to somewhere. At the same time, they have built too much steel capacity, leading to higher iron ore and coal prices, and a thinner margin for steel makers, and your local steel plant has to close. This is very different from when an individual or corporation makes an investment decision in a capitalist country. Because when they do it, they do it based on rational economic logic. It does not always work, but because the right incentives are in place, it usually does, and value is not bound to be destroyed. Capitalism.

Trading freely with China has effectively made communism the dominant global economic system for the allocation of scarce resources. This is what capitalism is supposed to be good at and communism really bad at. Yet, communism is gradually displacing capitalism in the global trading system.

FIGURE 6 - CHINA'S SHARE OF THE GLOBAL DEMAND FOR KEY COMMODITIES

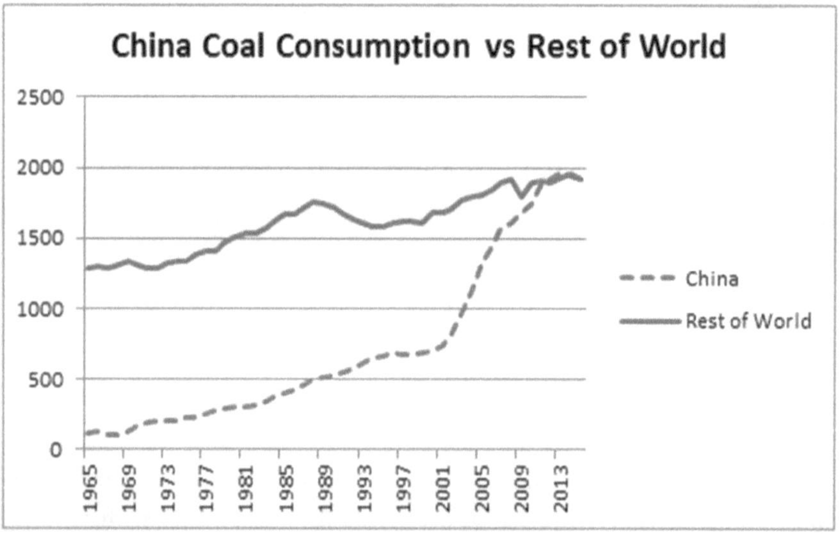

China Coal Consumption vs Rest of World

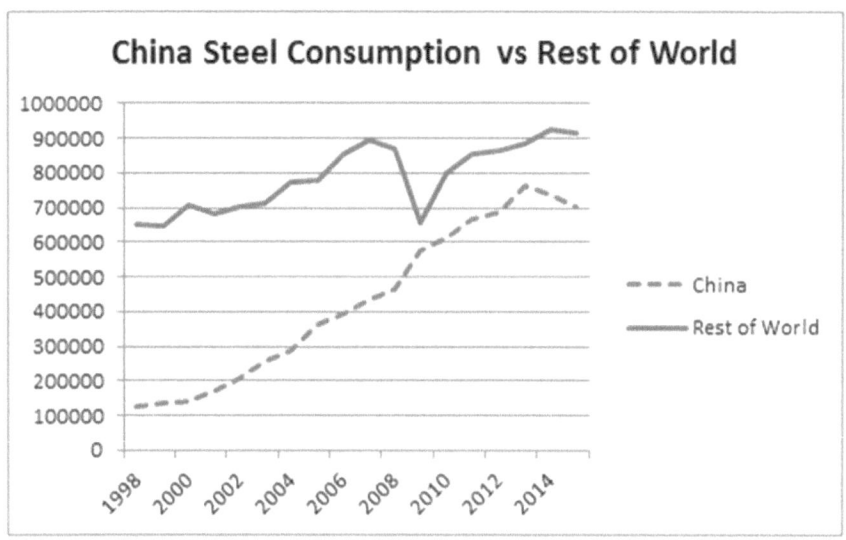

(Source: Author from Bloomberg data (million metric tons))

And that is just the tip of the iceberg.

I know, it sounds really surprising, and it similarly surprised me when I first came to the realization a number of years ago. But it's true – false (or simply naïve) economic "liberals", in their zeal to open up trade with as many nations as possible, have created a global trading system in which a communist party has become the dominant player.

It looks contradictory; it's like saying that the Pope doesn't believe in God, or that Windows never crashes, but as I will elaborate, it is incredibly self-evident once you realize what the Chinese are trying to sell and what that implies.

This is because false economic "liberals", as opposed to real ones, have built their entire narrative on the negation of the basic law of supply and demand.

Consider the basic justification of free trade with China, which they say will ultimately raise living standards in all participating countries. This is an assertion that completely ignores economic theory and the fact that true free trade cannot exist with a communist entity that operates as a monopoly, with extremely high levels of coordination between governments and its several public/"private" corporations.

Moreover, basic supply and demand also tells you that if your global economy suddenly receives 1 billion new, relatively underpaid, workers, the living standards of workers across the globe will gradually but inevitably decline. It won't matter whether the labour market is unionized or free, whether your population is highly educated or poorly educated, or whether your government is "right wing" or "left wing".

It is exactly this kind of obviously unrealistic assertion that is killing the credibility of the economic theory and economics as a profession today. If you think about what has been happening in our countries over the past few years, you can see that this credibility has already been seriously eroded. How much time do we have left until economics becomes irreversibly laughable in the eyes of the public, and follows the flat-earth hypothesis and the divine right of kings onto the trash heap?

Even in the academic arena, often the last hold-out of any pie-in-the-sky lack of realism, there is growing realization that this entire agenda has failed miserably. (The China Shock: Learning from Labour Market Adjustment to Large Changes in Trade - http://www.nber.org/papers/w21906)

Yet many of the economists who misrepresent "liberal" economics will cite economic theory as their justification, much as a religious fanatic would cite her view of God or a communist would cite Marx.

Having studied economics and finance to postgraduate level, I have watched as these ideologues have tried to cherry pick the parts that appear to support their unrealistic policies while ignoring the main body of knowledge and evidence that proves them logically wrong.

This is a lot like those sad periods of history when people selectively picked parts of large bodies of works, such as the Bible, to justify acts such as genocide and racism that are generally counter to the main idea of the book.

Unfortunately, this snake-oil economic "science" is repackaged as "the truth" for the people who want to sell this ideology to the world, and then spread by journalists and the media, and other people who either haven't studied economics in detail or slept during class, as "the established theory of economics".

This is then used as a "scientific" justification to all who have legitimate doubts about it based on the sheer observation of reality as they seek to explain away increasingly obvious signs of the failure of their theory. This is where ideologies such as communism and these false economic "liberals" present similarities to the organized religion of the Middle Ages. They all want to paper over the blatantly obvious to justify their dangerous departure from reality to an ideal world which is "better" according to their own twisted minds. Essentially, the denial of reality on the promise of an unrealistic "paradise".

These guys are still fighting the ideological battles of the early 1900s. At our expense.

What worries me most is that this misrepresentation of true liberal economics for ideological reasons puts at risk the very things that are indeed liberal economics and are in fact the basis for a prosperous society. As these people continue to manipulate the argument for the sake of their own ideology, we get increasingly close to a general backlash that discredits the good together with the bad. This was essentially what happened in the 1930s, which led to the rise of communism and extreme nationalism.

Freedom of choice, when investing and consuming. An efficient banking system and financial market. Equality of opportunity. A well-functioning job market. Rational international trade and investment flows. A free market. Non-discrimination in hiring and purchasing. A system of checks and balances at both the economic and political level.

These are things that have been proven over and over again to raise living standards. Indeed, they were the engine of the significant rise in living standards we experienced in the developed world over the past two centuries. This was especially true in the decades immediately after World War II, a period in which the gradual breakdown of the trade barriers and monopolies imposed by the European and Japanese empires led to an unprecedented improvement in overall living standards across the non-communist world.

Notice, by the way, that this was a period in which there was no major communist trading entity participating in the global capitalist trading system. Furthermore, none of the mistakes that the Soviet communists made, inefficient and disastrous as they may have been, wrecked the economies of the world in the ways the Chinese Communists have been allowed to in recent decades.

This was a major factor behind the success of global trade as a driver of the improvement of living standards during the 1940s-1990s. And a major reason for its failure ever since.

There are many reasons to be optimistic about the future. Seriously.

The past couple of decades fundamentally changed the general mood of our societies, from the optimistic nature of the 1980s and 1990s to our gloomy current self. I might have sounded despondent at times in this discussion; however, I want to emphasize that what was discussed here should not be viewed in a melancholy light.

Of course, what happened to us in the past two decades is really bad.

The death of the middle class. The increasing frequency of financial crises and bubbles in the world. The slowdown of economic growth and productivity. A global trading system that is increasingly under the influence of Communist China which was too small an economy to make a difference until the mid-1990s, as our previous charts have shown. But is now increasingly dominant.

But the way I see it, it is incredibly easy to go back to the path of prosperity. If you are doing a couple of things that are extremely harmful but the system is otherwise set up in a relatively rational way, all you have to do is to stop doing the incredibly bone-headed stuff. This is the major difference between us today and Soviet communism or even pre-revolution France.

Remove the trading policies that have wrecked the proper functioning of global capitalism, and it would resemble heavy rain in Death Valley. As the Chinese Communist Party would have it - a thousand flowers will blossom at once!

This is even easier than stopping digging when you're already in a hole (in which case you would only remain deep inside the hole). No, this is much simpler. It's like dropping an unnecessary load from your back. Drop it and you will feel lighter. And run faster. It should be immediate.

This is much more obviously logical because once the smoke clears the truth is self-evident. And the ideologists are running out of smoke on trying to hide the increasingly obvious. Just like all the disastrous ideologues before them.

History, composed of a large variety of unstoppable, inevitable forces, has a way of inevitably exposing such crazy, unrealistic ivory-tower ideas.

This is much better than blaming all of our problems on people getting older, which, over the past 10,000 years, you may have noticed hasn't led to a decline in living standards. Or technological innovation – clearly another threat to mankind's standards of living, having been wrecking it since we lived in caves with no electricity and no cars. How about technological innovation being too slow, despite the fact that some of the best generations lived in a relatively technologically stagnated 1960s and 1970s? Or global trade, which used to work quite well for the vast majority of the population as long as you didn't have a large communist party in control of most of it?

None of these overcomplicated "explanations" for the problem that is staring everyone in the face is up to the task of explaining why China is the dominant cause of them rather than an accessory or consequence of a much more serious problem.

The truth is, many of these explanations are dismal in the sense that they see our current predicament as something we cannot do anything about. For instance, the "demographic" view has an implicit assumption that the path towards population ageing and later marriages is structural and irreversible; similarly for the technology-based excuses.

For once, the truth is much more beautiful. We can do something about it. More than that, we, collectively, *will* almost inevitably change it. The question is how, and what will we have to sacrifice for it.

Human history is unforgiving. Any system that is perceived as failing to advance standards of living for the next generation is judged as inadequate by its own people and thrown out. Think of everything from the previous version of Chinese communism (the one that ran until the 1980s) to the old Soviet communism, or to the last years of Franco's Spain or pre-revolutionary Mexico.

This is what could or could not be different in our case, because the political and economic systems we currently have in the developed world are mostly worth saving. Think about how we have managed to slowly move past racial and gender discrimination, or how we are managing to create cities where the threat of common physical violence is the exception rather than the rule. However, you can bet that most of that will be lost together with the bad if we reach breaking point. Remember also that these things tend to happen much faster than us mere mortals like to think when we are in the middle of it. Think of the collapse of the Soviet Union.

We need to fix this before we lose our way of life to some kind of political backlash from one of the extremes, either the extremist right that will outlaw all foreign trade, good or bad, or the extremist left, that will seek to control wages and prices as much as the Soviets did.

One thing I want to emphasize is the danger of the other side of the spectrum – the so-called "socialists". They are right to be worried by all the problems that the common people are currently facing, from low housing affordability to income inequality, youth unemployment and the decline of the middle class. What is problematic in their solution is their emphasis on what I would call internal "redistribution" policies.

Our current problem permeates the entire society. You can't solve it by taxing the rich and giving to the poor. The rich will just use their immense resources to find a loophole and drop all their cash in the most lenient country available.

You can see this happening already, right? Robbing Peter to pay Paul won't work. The problem is not the fact that your brother might have a better room than you. It's the fact that guys from out of town are screwing you, your brother, your neighbours and your entire country. If you try to pursue this kind of internal redistribution of money without addressing the massive root causes behind it, all you will end up with is more internal conflict and even less ability to address the real issue.

Trying to solve our problems with handouts is creating a group of frustrated people who feel useless. And another group of people who feel that these guys, who were in fact mostly impacted by stupid economic policies completely outside of their control, are parasites and should be cut off. It's bad for everyone, and even worse when you don't even need to have all of these problems.

Because as I have tried to explain, this inequality is not something that is naturally, inevitably occurring, as many in both the socialist and false "liberal" camps would tell you (yes, they agree on something; in fact, they agree on many things – all of which are wrong).

Indeed, for most of the past century inequality was naturally falling, in an environment of constant improvement in standards of living! It is only rising now because of the way the developed world chose to engage trading with China, and to a less extent trading with other poor countries.

Ultimately, in our shared human experience, there are certain things that make the difference between societies that successfully address their problems and those that have ended up with severe internal conflicts, shooting at each other instead of at the real enemies. Those that have tried to solve their problems by seeking to somehow redistribute money inside their societies ended up in the brother-killing-brother camp. Those that have tried to solve their problems by either making their problems other countries' problems (like the British Empire in the past or Communist China today), or by pursuing genuine innovation (like the US or Japan in the 20th century), have done much better.

The US solved mass poverty by perfecting the old Venetian idea of the assembly line. The Soviets tried to solve it by imposing a totalitarian communist state that made private property illegal and redistribution compulsory. You can see the difference in the results.

We could be like Japan in the 1870s, or the European societies after the financial crises of the late 1800s, or the Spanish after Franco, with our societies adapting in a relatively organized way. Or we can get there after several major countries elect the far right or the far left in one or two general elections from now, and maybe a civil war here and there. History will get there inevitably; the question is how.

As I have said, I am not a big fan of using statistics to elaborate the obvious. My goal here is to write a book for normal human beings. I believe that statistics have been misused too much and for far too long to obfuscate the truth instead of exposing it. So I will try to follow the style of the original liberal economist, Adam Smith, and make arguments that are inherently logical and come from self-evident facts rather than throwing numbers around. Economics began to deviate from the real world back in the 1920s, when nationalists and communists were fighting in the streets, and everyone was trying to prove something to someone about the world. This was exactly the same period of time when economists began to ignore plain logic in favour of increasingly complicated statistical models, which, as any good economist knows, can be easily played around with to give you the result you want just by changing how you select, collect and process the data. Of course, being economists, they will probably say that the guys who disagree with them are the ones doing the data mining.

Before we address the elephant in the room, I want to briefly touch on what the "explanations" and "solutions" that have been floated and tried, repeatedly and without success, over the past few years, since things really start becoming so obviously out of whack.

Government spending or "fiscal stimulus". Monetary policy – like lowering interest rates and "QE". "Reforms". The role of technology. Demographics – people generally getting older. And last but not least, inequality.

I felt that it was better to discuss these "established" theories, which have failed us so miserably in the past few years, at the back of the book, and jump straight into what I think are the right issues to address. But I invite those that feel strongly about them to read those chapters to understand why they tend to be logically and practically flawed either as an explanation of cause and effect, or as a potential solution.

In the next sections we will examine in detail what I have alluded to are the real causes of the problem.

REAL CAUSE 1: TRADE WITH LOW WAGE COUNTRIES IS KNOWN TO THE ESTABLISHED ECONOMIC THEORY TO HARM WORKERS IN DEVELOPED COUNTRIES, THE OPPOSITE OF WHAT THE MEDIA WOULD DESCRIBE AS "LIBERAL" ECONOMICS...

Trade, division of labour, and how they have been misrepresented to justify the opposite of what they are supposed to involve

Trade is good. In its purest form, trade is an expression of the division of labour. You love cooking and your cousin loves fixing things. You could fix your own stuff and he could cook his own meals, but neither of you would be as good or as productive as you would be doing what you are particularly good at.

You become a great cook and cook for both of you. He fixes your things in addition to his, in exchange for your tasty dishes. More dishes, more fixing – everyone is better off.

FIGURE 7 - TRADITIONAL ECONOMIC MODEL OF DIVISION OF LABOUR

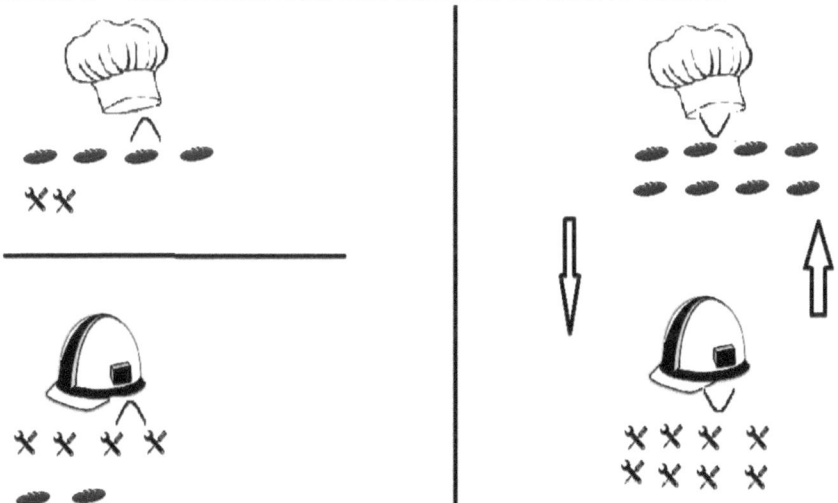

Division of labour is an essential part of human civilization, and indeed of what makes us human. So trade between individuals in the same society and living in close proximity is undeniably good.

The framework of economics follows a similar approach when it comes to trade. In the form where it makes most sense, it relates to natural advantages that are nearly impossible to replicate in a sensible business manner. Let's say Honduras is really good at making bananas and Chile is really good at walnuts. Same principle. Honduras could try to plant walnuts but that would take a lot of work and effort. Chile's landscape is mostly unsuitable for banana production. They specialize in what they are good at. They trade. The total number of bananas and walnuts available for both countries therefore increases so they can split the difference.

FIGURE 8 - BASIC ECONOMIC MODEL OF INTERNATIONAL TRADE IN END-PRODUCTS

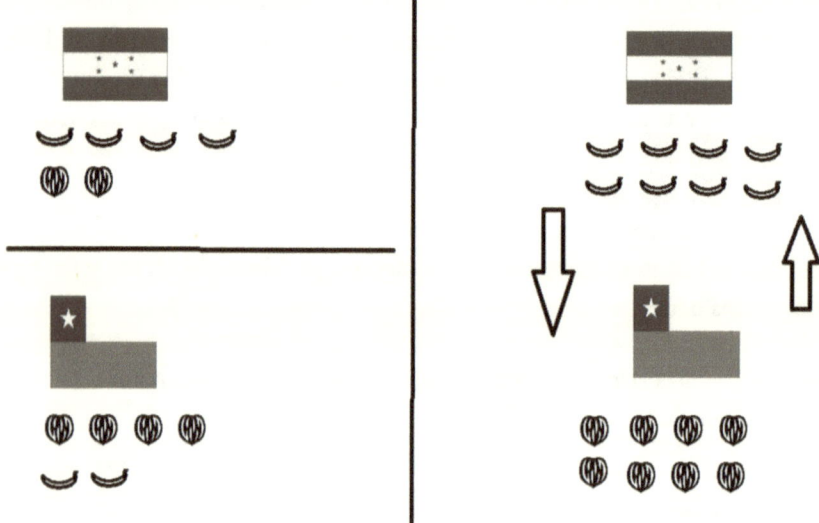

When it comes to supply and demand, if people like bananas as much as walnuts, then the price of bananas goes down in Chile, because it used to cost 2 walnuts to buy a banana and now it only costs 1. There are just more bananas in supply in Chile.

Let's keep that in mind. Looks like everyone is better off in Chile. People eat more bananas in Chile, and more walnuts in Honduras. Supply and demand balances, thus the price of bananas in Chile goes down.

There is usually a side discussion here regarding unemployment and whether if there is too much in one country, there are benefits from growing bananas or walnuts beyond those that are purely economic, or if the banana producers in

Chile will be screwed; however, I will try to sidestep this for now. Of course, the banana producers in Chile will have to close down but the benefits are so massive for the country that you can live with that. In fact, why protect these fat cats when people can just eat more bananas and be merrier? And could it be true that if unemployment in Chile is massive, maybe they are better off getting these people to grow some bananas and stop trading?

However, these arguments usually come from the other side – the socialists, who say that liberal economics doesn't take into account all variables or that the models are unrealistic. I accept all that.

But my goal here is not to show how the other side could be right.

It is instead to show that the theory of liberal economics itself shows that what these misrepresented "liberal economists" are pushing is some kind of very doubtful snake oil.

Here is where most so-called liberal economists like to stop and simply say that "economic theory shows that trade is unambiguously good for everyone" and if you don't understand it you are dumb, a communist or worse, and let's move on to the next topic…

Unless you are a banana in Chile.

Now, of course bananas have no feelings. And if you are a worker, you are just better off given the lower prices and higher real income.

So how could you be the banana? You are the banana if you are the one that is being competed out of the economic arena with a lower priced substitute.

You don't understand how liberal economics can show that trading with a country where people make one tenth of what you do will raise your standards of living? That's because it doesn't. It shows the opposite.

What these economists don't like to mention is that when you introduce an economic model that discusses the implications of trade for what are called workers (labour) and capital, the initial conclusion of "everyone is better off" does not apply under realistic conditions.

In the real world, national economies are more complex than just bananas and walnuts. You have a myriad of different products. If you are a worker, you may work in a car plant, a restaurant, or on a building site. If you are a truck or a metal-bashing machine, you can be similarly employed in multiple sectors.

These are what economists call "factors of production" – the things that are used to produce stuff.

Almost by definition, the so-called "developed" countries are richer because, throughout history, they have accumulated a relatively larger amount of wealth nationwide, which can be in the form of machinery, vehicles, buildings, roads, and all other forms of accumulated "capital" that can be used to facilitate the production of things.

This is what is called "capital intensity" – roughly how much the average worker of a country has of physical and financial capital to work with. It has been well documented by statisticians that capital intensity is a key driver of worker productivity and therefore standards of living (see for instance: "Why Do Some Countries Produce So Much More Output per Worker than Others?" by Robert Hall and Charles Jones).

It is also very intuitive. We can understand that people in a "poor" country with the same tools, same level of infrastructure, same minimum level of education necessary for the job and the same motivation as those in a developed country will produce the same. Ultimately what you can produce is the key driver of what you can earn. American education may be a little better than the Chinese system, but you can see that on education levels alone, it would be a stretch to justify why a worker in the US still makes more than eight times what a worker in China does in actual dollars.

The major reason why you have a TV, running water, electricity and other comforts is because you have accumulated all of this capital over the years to help you leverage your work for much better productivity than the guy who came from a country with much less "capital" and who may even be on a boat, plane or bus right now trying to immigrate to a rich country.

Now take a look at what the established theory of liberal economics has to say about when your country trades with his country.

FIGURE 9 - BASIC ECONOMIC MODEL OF THE IMPACT OF INTERNATIONAL TRADE ON FACTORS OF PRODUCTION SUCH AS LABOUR AND CAPITAL

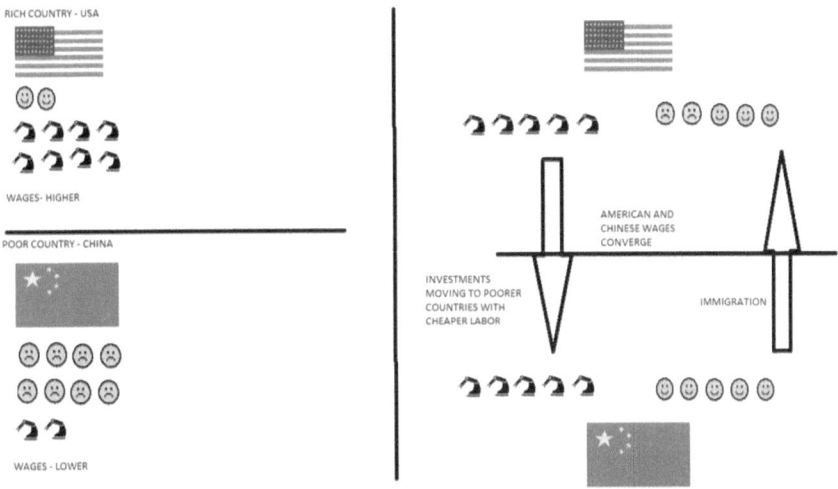

Obviously, like everything that involves large groups of people, this will be true only in general terms. You will still have some guy from the US moving to China because his specific job can be done better there, or the occasional Chinese company that will need to do business in the US for some specific reason. Or some Chinese guys who will want to buy some condos in Manhattan (or buy the New York Yankees) to put their money in a safer country. The Chinese might even buy a company here.

But look around you and you will see that the general trend holds firmly in the real world. For example, brand-new manufacturing plants are rarely built in developed countries by Chinese companies. Labour is much scarcer there than in their home country. Supply and demand.

Yes. This is *the* established liberal economic theory that says it is absolutely natural and logical to expect wages to fall in a rich country when it trades with a poor country. Which should not surprise you, even with all the clueless journalists repeating what some false "liberal economists" said about the established liberal economic theory, preaching that "trade should benefit all countries".

This is also called the balance of supply and demand – the basis of all economic liberalism. Remember, "comrade"?

One country has a lot of labour and not much capital (a "poor country"). It trades with a country with a lot of capital and proportionally less labour (a "rich country"). This increases the supply of labour in the system. Therefore the price of labour – aka wages – goes down in the rich country.

By the way, you can see from the above that even if you manage to completely close your country to immigration, total free trade with a much poorer country will gradually but eventually lead to a similar outcome – a process where the standards of living of the two countries converge. So free trade with a poorer country is almost the same as free immigration from a poorer country. An increase in supply of workers in the system decreases the price of that labour (wages). Again, just supply and demand. Self-evident. Common sense. Capitalism.

Trade with China is like exporting capital and importing 1bn workers into your economy. The economic impact is not so different from having them arrive at your country and work from there. And once again, you would expect that to lead to a massive increase in the supply of workers and therefore a fall in wages, wouldn't you? Supply and demand.

This is one thing that everyone who studied international economics knows but no one likes to talk about. You are now grasping how a supposedly scientific and neutral economist community selectively ignores the stuff that is not in line with their crazy and ideological concept of a "global crusade for good".

Hello banana man!

What happens when everyone wins?

So now we have TWO impacts. Trade with a poor country like China would indeed lower product prices. But it would also hit wages relative to the remuneration of other factors of production, like capital. One is positive, the other one negative. Which one prevails?

Once again, we can see how common sense and logic have long been neglected by so-called financial journalists and those that call themselves free market economists.

In real-life economics, there are many things that will affect the conclusion, from how close a country is to another one (think of Mexico and the US) or whether they specialize in generally similar products (like Japan and Germany).

But the key variable, as is clearly laid out and intuitive, is the difference in general levels of per person wealth, wealth here being a general term for machinery, technology, infrastructure etc., also known as "capital intensity".

Let's think of the two extreme cases here.

When the US trades with a relatively rich or advanced country (like Germany or Japan for instance), the first model prevails. For the sake of argument, you initially had companies making crappy cars in the US and crappy software in Germany. Now, because you have trade and more competition, cars in the US are better, even the US car manufacturers that have remained had to shape up and produce much better cars, and in fact German and Japanese car manufacturers invested heavily in factories inside the US to serve the local markets. At the same time, software in Germany is much better than before.

As you can see, when it comes to trade with China, the game changes. They are not innovating. They are not proposing different business models or technologies or better design. They are not building many new plants in the US.

The only thing they are doing is undercutting the labour force in the US. They might build one plant here or there but in general terms rarely do so, simply because workers in their home country are so much cheaper. This trade will lead to lower prices but not necessarily much better products. And because the first effect (lower prices, more competition) is vastly dwarfed by the second (the significant deterioration of the supply and demand balance for labour and wages), we have a serious impact on the standards of living of the average worker.

To illustrate the argument, think of it like this:

FIGURE 10 - WHEN INTERNATIONAL TRADE CAN BE BENEFICIAL, OR NOT

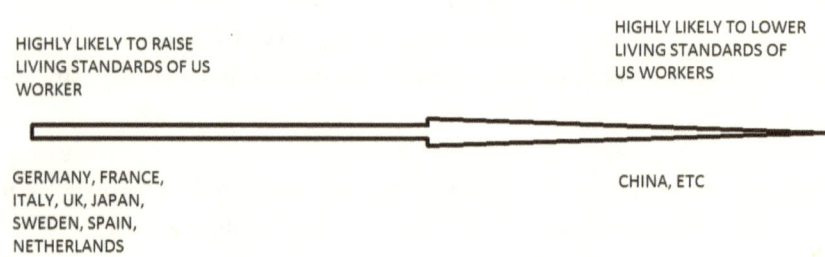

TRADE IS

HIGHLY LIKELY TO RAISE LIVING STANDARDS OF US WORKER

HIGHLY LIKELY TO LOWER LIVING STANDARDS OF US WORKERS

GERMANY, FRANCE, ITALY, UK, JAPAN, SWEDEN, SPAIN, NETHERLANDS

CHINA, ETC

This is a well-established conclusion for anyone who studied the impact of international trade on the market for factors of production – in this case workers.

So please do not trust anyone that bashes capitalism, real economic liberalism and economic science as the source of all modern problems. As you can see, liberal economic theory is on the same side as you.

It also says that trading freely with extremely poor countries can be a bone-headed idea.

Now let's try to understand these false economic "liberal" people. Why do they say that trade should ultimately benefit almost everyone and all countries? It is not such a daft idea as it first appears. Let me try to explain why.

This is because the first model, the banana-walnut model, was devised around three centuries ago, when the standard of living of a peasant in England wasn't that much better than his equivalent in China. So the massive differential in levels of per person capital and wealth was not particularly relevant at the time. As you can see, in today's world it is highly relevant.

This is also because free trade actually delivered a massive boost to standards of living during the post-World War II period. The world was previously dominated by colonial monopolies everywhere with almost no trade between them, which was bad for everyone. But then the end of WW II unleashed a wave of market openings and more trade, from Germany to Italy, France, Japan, Canada, the UK, the US and others, that significantly contributed to better standards of living pretty much everywhere.

So this is what economists say when they say that trade is not a zero-sum game and that everyone wins – peace and love, etc. Unfortunately, this argument has been used to hide the truth instead of defending good trade from harmful trade.

Now look at this chart and see if you can see the difference between the period when trade was helping the standards of living of developed countries and when it started to hurt.

FIGURE 11 - SHARE OF WORLD EXPORTS OF US, JAPAN AND GERMANY VERSUS CHINA

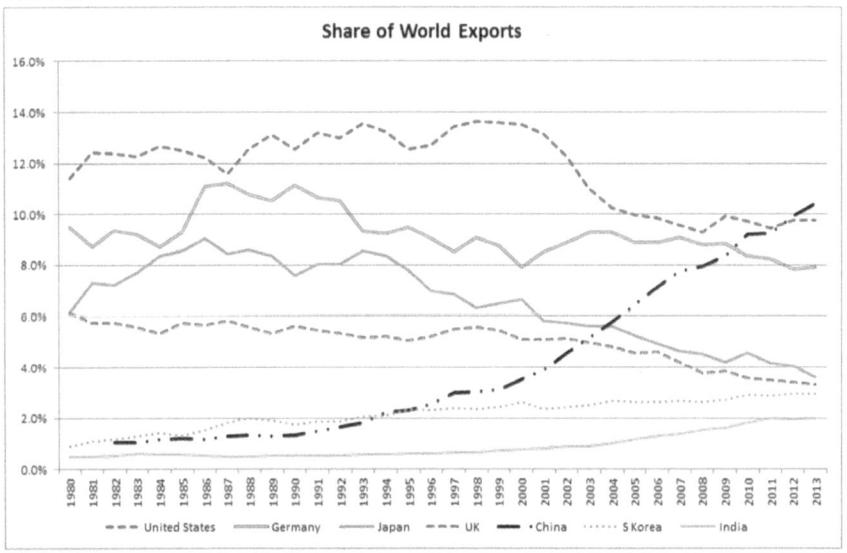

(Source: Author aggregation of international trade statistics)

Once again, we can see how our basic logical economic model is correct. When trade is mainly between developed countries, it is beneficial. As soon as a country like China, with cheap labour, starts getting a massive share of the pie, your standards of living start going down. It is worrying that no one in the established media has tried to talk about this, as it is something that has been clear and self-evident for quite some time now.

And another key difference: there was no major communist country operating inside the global capitalist trading system during the immediate post-war period, as the Soviet bloc was mostly closed to trade. I will discuss later how the presence of a large communist country such as China in the global trading system effectively changes the way the entire system works.

So when you trade with countries that have a history of technological advancements, have the ability to develop advanced technology, have a decent amount of wealth themselves, then it's good. Otherwise, trade can, in many cases, be harmful to the workers of the rich countries.

Great, so we have good trade, whose continued existence is being threatened by the growth of bad trade. The blind "liberal economist" ideologists want the bad trade to continue, but what they are risking is that this will continue until workers in developed countries get so fed up with everything that they throw all trade, good and bad, on the trash heap, together with all of the other stuff that really is good and makes a difference for us, like a free banking system, competition, efficient labour markets, a strong financial market, maybe even our political systems.

Tom Clancy himself would never have thought of a more powerful way to destroy capitalism and spread communism around the world.

Of course, we already instinctively knew all of this. This is because we are human beings living on planet Earth. Unfortunately, the minds of ideologically blinded people tend to wander into strange and faraway places in the universe. I am just trying to show you that even the theory of liberal economics actually shows that these people live in cloud-cuckoo land.

How about inequality? Here you can see why it is not the result of some perverse conspiracy by some evil Wall Street bankers arranged inside strip clubs. It is just that the decision to trade with poor countries hit the people who draw most of their income from their wages, and benefitted those that draw most of their income from the wealth they already have. The workers group is by no means just janitors and maids, people! Lower-wage people might get hit harder at first but that group will eventually be everyone from lawyers to engineers and teachers to steel workers. They may have higher qualifications, but that does not completely insulate them, remember? It is not highly educated people benefit – less educated people suffer. It's all workers, rich and poor, highly qualified or less qualified, ultimately taking a hit from the massive deterioration of the supply and demand balance of workers in the economy.

Now, I don't have the exact numbers here, but you can see that the labour group - ie the people that derive more income from their wealth than they do from their work - will probably be the vast majority of the population, certainly above 90%, and the capital group will probably be a very small number.

The "1 percenters". Sound familiar? Isn't that beginning to look much more like the world you see around you when you look out your window?

Of course, also because of the way that trade works, the people who are lucky enough to have professions that are close to the people with capital would benefit, like Ferrari dealers, high-end jewellers, or even people like me in financial markets. But of course the rest of the population is worse off.

So you see? Inequality. No conspiracy; well, maybe a little communist conspiracy – a gift from our comrades in the Chinese Communist Party. But mostly just the dumb way in which our societies decided to approach international trade.

So, as I said before, you can either try to solve inequality by trying to tax the richer people, in which case you could have a civil war at one point. Because hey you never know, they start with the Ferrari-driving guys, but then they start going down to anyone who has a two-storey house, and then down further. Or you can solve inequality by reconsidering this false dogma, which is being unfairly blamed on economic liberalism and the theory of economics.

So be warned about these economists who say that their science points to the undeniable conclusion that free trade with everyone is great. These people are ideologically driven. They want to forget that they ever saw what I have shown you above. But that's how it works. Because it is the natural and inevitable consequence of the simple law of supply and demand that guides capitalism. If you reject this, you reject capitalism. And then you are no better than some Soviet apologist.

So the next time they try to justify an imbecilic course of action by invoking the established science of economics, as if they were invoking the seventh commandment of Moses, rest assured.

It is not economics that is idiotic.

It is not capitalism that is inhumane or narrow minded.

It's just that these people who misrepresent liberal economics don't know what they are talking about.

REAL CAUSE 2: ...AND CHEAP LABOR KILLS INNOVATION

When there is lots of cheap labour, you don't innovate, because there is no need. You can hire someone to do the job. When there is no labour around, or it is expensive, you need to invent a machine to do it.

Let's continue down this path. You might find this ironic but it has not occurred to many in the economist profession that <u>sustainably</u> increasing the value of labour relative to everything else is the main driver of what we would call economic development.

By sustainably I mean not by artificially raising prices, like mandating an excessively high level of minimum wage or incentivizing heavy unionization and strikes. This kind of stuff just takes from one brother to give to another, and makes the country as a whole worse off because it is a deviation from the "win-win" economic optimum.

By sustainably, I mean raising the relative scarcity of labour relative to other stuff via decisions on trade, savings and other economic policies. More investments in your country, less trade with countries that have an abundant supply of much cheaper labour.

Now think of the implications of making labour a relatively scarce resource. This is a process, which has been going on for the past 3,000 years at least, sometimes in a "two-step forward/one-step back" way. This is what took all of us from slavery to being peasants and treated like crap, to the current situation where people have rights, some purchasing power, and some ability to shape their own destiny. This happened not because of the kindness of the hearts of the initial slave owners back in the Roman Empire or Babylon. No, it happened because the gradual accumulation of wealth, technological advancements, and other tools of general economic progress led to a situation where workers became increasingly scarce relative to the other factors of production in the economy (land, machinery, financial capital, etc.). You can no longer simply pay people peanuts and take away their rights. You can no longer trade a slave for a horse, or for a plot of land. People are too scarce for that. Population has grown, but the accumulated wealth of the society increased by much more than that. Supply and demand.

Labour-saving technologies have raised overall standards of living because it makes the work of an individual more productive, makes labour scarcer relative to other production factors, and gives the worker more bargaining power to increase his own remuneration. Think of how much an air steward makes in a flight versus what a guy makes at McDonalds, for jobs that are not so radically different. In the case of the air steward, a relatively small number of them have the power to stop a highly capital-intensive value chain (via strikes and other actions), while the worker at McDonalds operates a much less capital-intensive process where he can be more easily replaced by another person in the event of a labour dispute.

Now some, especially those with a socialist bent, would say that technology that cuts the number of workers per task would lead to a huge decrease in wages. But that is the opposite to our entire shared experience of the evolution of economics, technology and human history since the Stone Age. Increasing the productivity of the average worker is what has made it possible for us to evolve to having to use almost our entire labour force to scrounge for food every day to be able to free some up to do other stuff such as trading, engineering, and other roles.

This process is ultimately the very definition of the evolution of mankind from subsistence to civilization. If the economy is set up in a capitalistic way, people who lose their jobs to technology are only temporarily affected. Both society as a whole and themselves gain in the grander scheme of things.

You can see that the "trade with China" model above would naturally lead to a reversal of this process of gradual labour scarcity, and therefore prevent economic development. It would lead to workers being more abundant versus the rest of the stuff in the economy. This is what has been happening over the past 20 years and is a key reason why standards of living have been stagnant or declining in developed economies.

Because what really took us from the Stone Age to where we are now are what we would call labour-saving technologies. From the invention of the wheel to railroads, the spinning wheel to the assembly line, and from the plough to the modern combine harvester, these are technologies, which have made it possible for us to raise our life expectancy from 25 years initially to 75 today.

But as with everything else in nature, evolution does not happen unless there is a need for it. If labour is relatively abundant in the economy, and capital is flowing out to societies where workers are much cheaper and more abundant, then you can see how over the medium term the speed of technological advancement, especially in terms of production process technology, will also stall in the most advanced societies.

This is a well-known process, which economic historians have observed. It is the reason why the Industrial Revolution started in Europe and not in China, even though China had a much bigger market, and initially even more advanced technology than Europe. The renaissance, the Black Death, and the discovery of the Americas led to a situation where workers were more scarce in Europe and therefore technological evolution paid off economically the significant costs of learning and disseminating new technologies. Supply and demand.

There are also the people that will tell you that innovation has not stopped over the past 30 years – they are right. iPhones and iPads and PlayStation4 right? But here is the confusion. What this "China trade" has slowed the most was process innovation, which is a key driver of improvements of standards of living (together with capital accumulation, as discussed). This is different from product innovation, like iPhones or the Toyota Prius. Product innovation was the automobile. But it remained an elite, highly expensive product destined for the few until the idea of applying the assembly line for its production process was implemented by people like Henry Ford.

Product innovation makes things available. Process innovation makes them affordable for the average person. Novelties that are not affordable... Look around you. Sound familiar? This is, not surprisingly, the world of today. Things are generally less affordable than before. By the way, that is what the chart on stagnating or declining household incomes shows as well.

Now, the silly people camp will say that trading with low wage countries such as China will make products affordable. But that's because they are silly. Yeah, prices are lower. But that does not mean that they are more affordable. As we have seen, what will go even lower is the remuneration of people who depend on their work for a living. So the purchasing power of workers in developed countries declines as a result of the system and of the economic model as well as of simple logic. Which, as we have seen, will ultimately be the dominant trend for everyone. Relative prices, remember? Supply and demand. Sure, initially it will just be the people that make the products that are being directly exposed and will get hit but then it gradually spreads to the rest of the economy. Because this is a shift in the supply and demand balance of workers as a whole. The guy who lost his job can compete for yours. Capitalism.

Indeed, as we showed before, this is exactly what has been happening. Remember that we are talking about *real* income (see figure 3), folks, which means your actual income adjusted by the prices you have to pay. See how much of a fudge this argument of "trading with China makes products more affordable" really is? Just as a reminder:

FIGURE 3 – REAL AVERAGE INCOME FOR THE BOTTOM 90% IN JAPAN, GERMANY, ITALY, UK, FRANCE, CANADA AND THE USA, 1950-2013.

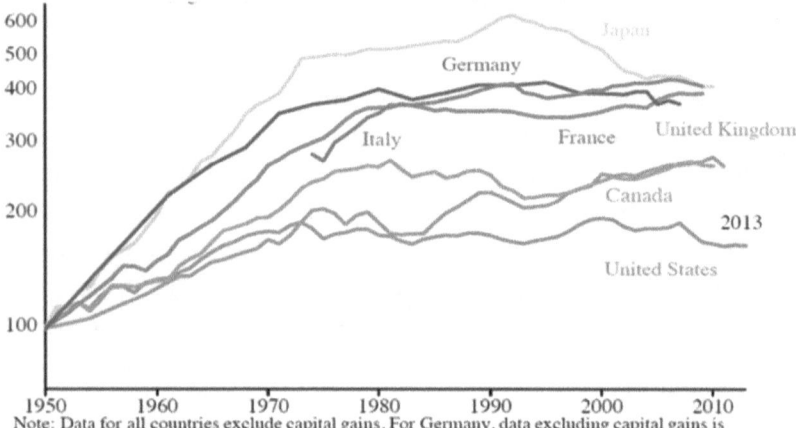

Note: Data for all countries exclude capital gains. For Germany, data excluding capital gains is unavailable after 1998, so this chart displays data including capital gains adjusted for the historical relationship between capital-inclusive and capital-exclusive incomes. Italian data begins in 1974 and is indexed to the average of the other series at that point. Italian data is calculated by CEA from the income level and share of the top 10 percent as provided by the World Top Incomes Database.
Source: World Top Incomes Database; Saez (2015); CEA calculations.

(Source: Council of Economic Advisers – 2015 Report to the President https://www. whitehouse.gov/administration/eop/cea/economic-report-of-the-President/2015)

Now we can understand one of the major reasons why there seems to have been a general downtrend in the growth rates of our economies over the past 20 years – the so-called "secular stagnation" (secular means through two or more business cycles). You can see that while these false "liberal" economists clamour to find the real causes behind this like headless chickens, blaming everything from a lower birth rate to less government spending or more government spending, they are simply afraid of getting outside of their ideological comfort zones to see answers straight in front of them.

When a country with a high capital to labour ratio ("rich") trades with a country with a low capital to labour ratio ("poor"), you should expect lower productivity growth in the rich country because productivity growth is mainly driven by increases in capital intensiveness, which as we have seen would fall if you add 1 billion workers to your economic system. Oh, and surprise surprise, that's exactly what is happening.

FIGURE 12 - LABOUR PRODUCTIVITY GROWTH IN THE MAJOR DEVELOPED ECONOMIES, 1950-2013.

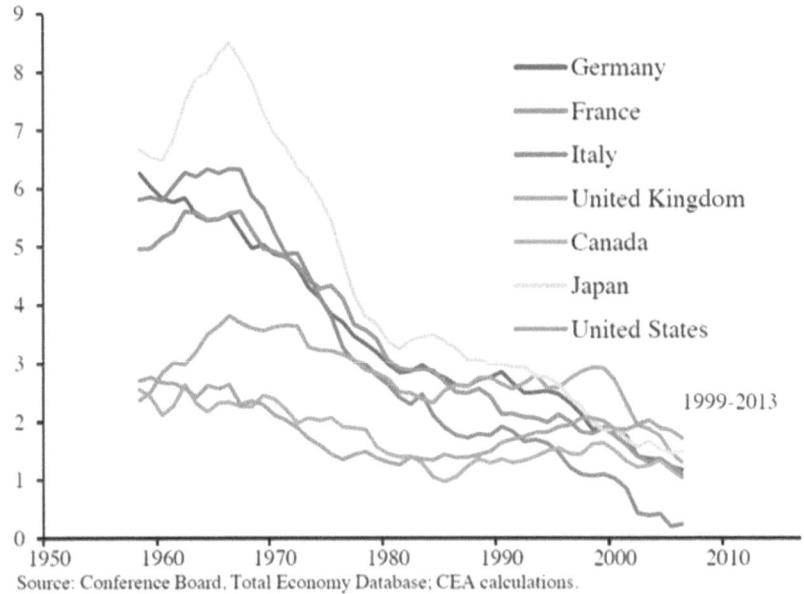

Source: Conference Board, Total Economy Database; CEA calculations.

(from Council of Economic Advisers – 2015 Report to the President https://www. whitehouse.gov/administration/eop/cea/economic-report-of-the-President/2015)

There is no point trying to overeducate people or make them do degrees that are not useful in modern society and do not lead to a job – this just leads to more student debt. Education does indeed increase labour productivity and the ability of an individual to be productive in any kind of job. However, like everything else in economics, or in nature for that matter, most of the impact is felt in the most basic levels of effort – i.e. teaching people how to read and write and the first eight years of basic education. You can see how there is a limit to that. Overeducating people will never make the people of one country ten times more productive than the people of another, poorer country that has a minimal level of organized basic education. This is what would be needed to maintain the current difference in terms of standards of living between developed and developing countries. Obviously this is not possible. Better education alone will not save the standards of living of the middle classes of the developed countries.

Forcing everyone in the US to do a PhD will therefore not stabilize the real median income of the population of the country.

Of course, for the owners of the financial capital, they are better off not being forced to innovate, compete and manage their companies properly. Why do all of that if they can just cross the border and get someone to do the same thing that you do for them for one tenth of the wages? But over the medium to long term, even they are not clear winners.

The labour-saving issue is also valid in the argument over mass immigration.

The most recent and blatant real-life example that I can think of in this context is how fruit and vegetable farms in the US reacted to the end of the Bracero migrant programmes back in the 1960s. After whining loudly that it would kill orange and tomato farms as labour would be too expensive, guess what? They are still around. They did not disappear. Look at what they did!

FIGURE 13 - HOW RESTRICTIONS ON CHEAP LABOUR IMMIGRATION LED TO A RISE IN INNOVATION AND MECHANIZATION OF FRUIT AND VEGETABLE FARMS IN THE US

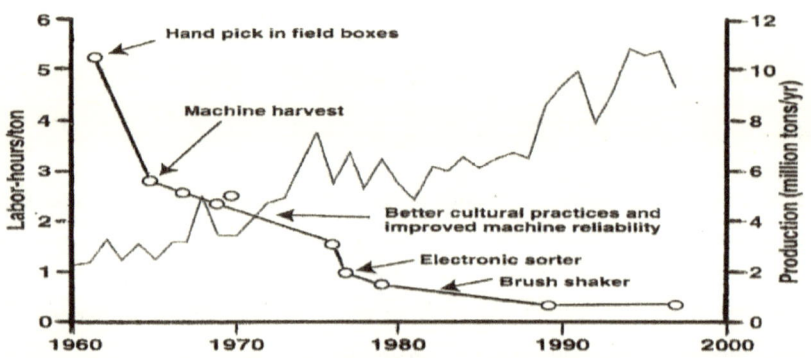

(Source: http://www.choicesmagazine.org/choices-magazine/theme-articles/immigration-and-agriculture/the-status-of-labour-saving-mechanization-in-us-fruit-and-vegetable-harvesting)

So no, farms did not disappear because cheap manual labour became less available, as in fact, they have not disappeared after 3,000 years of labour becoming increasingly scarcer, from the slave to the combine harvester.

The owners of these farms just got off their "fat, lazy asses" and invested in technology that would make it unnecessary to relay on a large army of poor, desperate people. They also changed the variety of fruits and vegetables they planted to make it easier for the machine to handle, and they organized labour in a way that would generally save it.

This is capitalism. This is innovation. Supply and demand.

You can see how throughout the economy this process has been curtailed. People used to lose jobs to mechanization, but to get even better and less boring jobs. The combine harvester came along and people no longer had to work all day in the fields, and were ultimately better off.

Not anymore. Jobs are no longer upgraded. They are just shipped off. We lost an entire generation of technological advancement by insisting on this foolishness.

So do not trust anyone who says that if you can't find a desperate person willing to work for peanuts in your country or in China to do what needs to be done, your economic system will collapse. Because this goes against every single case study of economic history and our shared 3,000 years of human history, as well as simple common sense. The system will not collapse. The system will evolve. Some jobs will be mechanized, others will disappear because there will be no more need for them. We will all be better off for it.

Being a full-time maid was the main form of female occupation in Victorian England. Female work was so cheap that even a lower-middle-class person could afford one or two full-time live-in maids. Fortunately, things in England and across Europe evolved to a point where human beings had a bit more economic value than that. But, of course, with mass immigration and full, free trade with much poorer countries, you can see how this process would have been slowed. Look around you and you will see how the policies discussed above also slowed the evolutions of the professions over the past few decades, especially in the services sectors, similar to what you would have expected. The evolution of how work is carried out in healthcare, restaurants and hotels has generally frozen at the level reached in the mid-1980s.

There are also many people saying, "Oh give up, manufacturing jobs will not come back, you can't turn back the clock" and other nonsense. Don't trust them either. Companies in developed countries would just react to labour being less abundant by mechanizing and upgrading jobs. Customer first! Adapt! Some low paid jobs would cease to exist, which is not bad as long as these jobs are upgraded and not simply shipped off. This is essential because this process of constantly upgrading jobs has pushed human society to develop over the past 3,000 years. This process is significantly retarded (thanks to wide-eyed, pie-in-the-sky economists) when you have a massive supply of low wage workers either via trade with poor countries or via massive immigration.

By the way, the entire industrialization process actually consisted of bringing jobs that were done in less advanced countries to more advanced countries! It was all about the textile mills of England displacing spinning wheels in India. Or think about when the assembly line was perfected by Ford for the auto industry. The US had some of the highest wages in the world at the beginning of the 1900s. Yet, the introduction of the assembly line, and major capital investments, triggered an early cost advantage that led the country to dominate the auto industry for most of the last century – further proof that, done right, mechanization can lead to even lower costs than simple reliance on low wages, especially in sectors that are less labour-intensive.

You can therefore see that the view that manufacturing will inevitably be a poor country's job is the opposite of our historical experience. In fact, the only period of modern history in which this has been the case was the freak period we have witnessed over the past two decades.

It also seems that having a sizeable manufacturing sector is the only consistent way to have a sizeable middle class, which is the basis of the entire Western civilization in its current form. That is because manufacturing remains the only sector that can allow a large number of people with an average but useful level of education to generate enough economic value to have a middle-class standard of living. You can see that. Think of our steel mill workers of the past versus our Walmart or McDonalds workers of today. Otherwise we will have what we are trending for currently, which is a small number of highly paid and overeducated professionals and a large number of poorly paid people in the services sector. We can't have an entire country of doctors or software engineers. It does not work like that. Israel tried! All you end up with is truckloads of university graduates overloaded with debt flipping burgers somewhere. Sound familiar?

The reason why only manufacturing can provide these middle class jobs, unless your country is blessed with a lot of land and not many people, like Australia or New Zealand, is as above: capital intensity. Only sectors where the developed countries can leverage their capital intensity can provide jobs that are internationally competitive on a sustained basis. An IT consultant in India can do the same job as a US IT consultant but at a fraction of the wages. You will have some high-end niches here and there where US IT guys will prosper, like the gaming industry, but as a general rule, US IT consulting will probably never be internationally competitive with the Indian IT sector. Software looks like a high tech sector but it is also very labour-intensive (as opposed to capital-intensive).

You see? Being high tech in a totally open trade regime is not what will protect standards of living in developed countries. The only thing that can do that, in such an environment, are capital-intensive sectors. Silicon Valley, Hollywood and Wall Street will always provide a small number of highly paid jobs but they will never be mass industries. That is because it is in practice impossible for any nation of at least medium size (Israel and Lebanon might be different) to rely only on these wealthy but niche sectors to support a broad middle class standard of living for their entire country. Of course, we all know this. Silicon Valley and Hollywood and Wall Street have prospered over the past 15 years yet we can see how it has made little difference to the middle class of the US as a whole.

REAL CAUSE 3: ECONOMICS HAS ESTABLISHED THAT YOU CANNOT HAVE REAL FREE TRADE WITH AN ENTITY THAT OPERATES AS A MONOPOLY. A COMMUNIST POLITICAL AND ECONOMIC SYSTEM OPERATES AS A MONOPOLY. TRADING WITH COMMUNIST CHINA IS THE OPPOSITE OF FREE TRADE.

Free markets are not compatible with a monopoly. A large communist trading country like China operates as a monopoly. So global capitalism cannot survive with China as part of the global trading system.

Even if low wage manufacturing remains part of the global trading system, there is massive benefit to be derived from redirecting it towards low wage countries that trade in a capitalistic, free market and honest way, like Mexico or Chile, instead of trading with Communist China, which employs every trick ever invented by man to manipulate the exchange rate, non-tariff trade barriers, and access to their own markets.

What I am going to show you next should raise the hairs on the back of your neck even more. Because I will show you that low wages are just the tip of the iceberg on how trade with China erodes the standards of living of all capitalist countries, and not just developed ones.

China being poor is not the only problem. It's not even the main problem.

What I described before was a process that would apply to China, but also to poorer countries like Mexico. And yet trading with all of Latin America, Africa and Southeast Asia did not have such a negative impact on the standards of living of developed countries back in 1945–1990s. So there must be something more, maybe much worse, behind all this.

In addition, most developing countries, including Mexico, have not fared as well as China over a longer period of time, so something must be going on here. Low labour costs have been a driver of negative change in the standards of living of developed countries but are not the only driver.

(Source: Author, elaboration of Bloomberg and international statistical data)

Take Mexico, for example. They are poorer traders than China but they are honest traders. Over most of the past two decades, they have derived an external deficit from their trade with the rest of the world. Most Latin America countries are like that. They don't steal much technology; they don't try to extract unreasonable commercial terms as a price to do business in their country; they don't force companies to give away technology or trade secrets as a price to sell into their country.

Even if your standards of living go down a bit by trading more freely with them, they are not an extortion racket disguised as a country.

This is because Mexico, or any other capitalist country (even dictatorships!), does not have the ability to reach a high level of coordination between the government, their individual states, and each of their companies. In fact, such behaviour would even be illegal, contravening anti-trust laws as well as others such as consumer protection laws. Telmex competes against Axtel, just like GM competes with Ford. And South Carolina competes with Alabama for their investment, like Coahuila and Nuevo Leon.

Now I want to show you two pictures of what economists think is a free market and what is not. It's OK, you don't need to understand. I just want

41

to show the framework of thinking of modern economists. These are just graphical, technical representations of common sense. Supply and demand.

The first one is a free market. There, if prices are too low, people buy more and companies produce less, and vice versa until supply and demand balances. At that point, the market clears. Trade benefits everyone, at a certain price and quantity that is determined collectively by the myriad of trades of the individual buyers and sellers; the welfare of the entire system is maximized.

The second one is a much darker situation. It happens when one producer, or a small number of producers acting in coordination, decide to interfere with the free market to extract benefits for themselves. In this simple example, they form a cartel to restrict supply and artificially raise prices. In real life, it can be anything from locking distribution channels, key technologies, operating licenses, or anything else that gives such agents the power to distort the outcome of the market to their own benefit. In such scenarios, prices are above what they would normally be in a free market, and the quantity supplied is lower. The producers win, the consumers lose, and as you would have expected, the system as a whole is worse off versus the previous case.

FIGURE 15 - PERFECTLY COMPETITIVE FREE MARKET VERSUS MONOPOLY – TECHNICAL REPRESENTATIONS

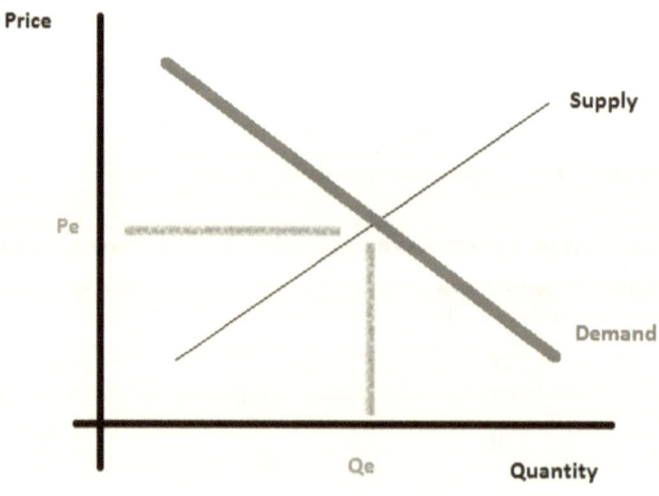

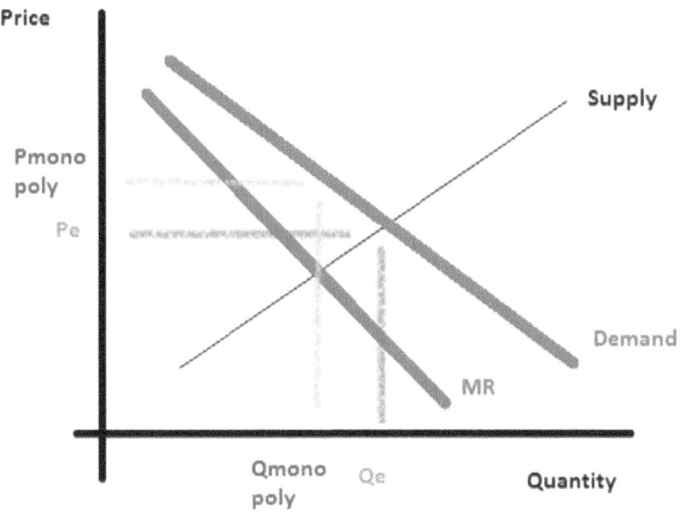

Price

Pmono
poly

Pe

Supply

Demand

MR

Qmono
poly

Qe

Quantity

(Source: Author)

The first chart shows an example of free markets in action; the second chart shows the opposite, i.e. monopolistic forces distorting the market.

Even the false "liberals" recognize this. This is why you have antitrust regulators everywhere in the world today, looking at every major corporate merger and at every major market – which is a good thing. Everyone understands that unless you have a very strong reason for it, allowing the formation of companies that will have a disproportionate amount of power in the market is harmful for society as a whole.

You have less competition. You have higher prices. You have crappier products or services. You have less innovation. My way or the highway – this is the choice that they can impose on the rest of the economy.

Think of what economists would call more generally "monopoly power". This is not just the simplistic idea of charging higher prices for a lower quantity of goods. Rather it's when an agent is big and powerful enough to perversely distort the competitive field in their favour. For instance, Walmart can charge lower prices for goods of a comparable quality to other suppliers – initially, before they kill off all that is left of the local competition – and then can potentially give you the same low prices but much lower quality thereafter – and also pay their employees like crap. Or think of Apple iTunes, or the new Microsoft Windows, which is supposedly given for "free" in its latest edition…

And as economists are well aware, you don't need a 90% market share to have a power monopoly. For instance, in the UK, a business with more than 25% market share is considered by the government to have "monopoly power". This makes sense. In a market where there are a lot of small guys, one guy with a 25% market share can dominate the market, and make everyone else dance to their own tune and change their entire businesses to adapt and survive.

FIGURE 16 - WALMART'S MARKET SHARE IN THE US, 2014 – HOW A TRADING PARTY CAN HAVE A SIGNIFICANT INFLUENCE IN THE MARKET EVEN WITH A 25% MARKET SHARE

Market share of the leading grocery retailers in the United States in 2014

This statistic shows the market share of the leading grocery retailers in the United States in 2014. In that year, Walmart captured the highest market share in the U.S. food retail sector with about 24.5 percent.

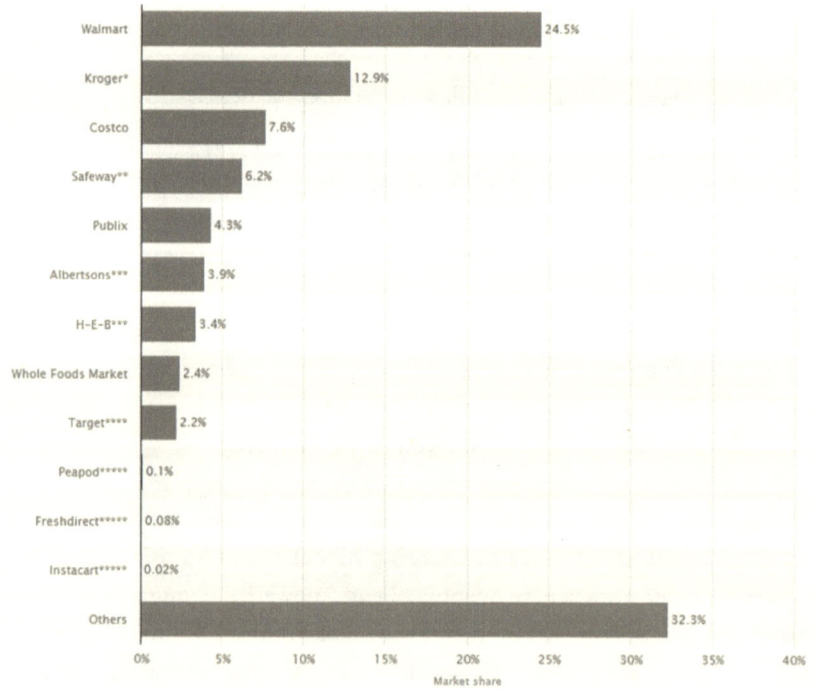

© Statista 2016

(Source: http://www.statista.com/statistics/240481/food-market-share-of-the-leading-food-retailers-of-north-america/)

This is why the proposed AT&T/T-Mobile merger was blocked. This is why the old AT&T telecoms monopoly was broken up in the first place in the US, remember? This is why the Standard Oil anti-trust case came up all those years back. And think about Windows ("damn my computer crashed again"). Or if you only have one grocery store in your neighbourhood. They can sell you crap products, but if they take away your choice, you still have to go to them, right?

You therefore have to guess what kind of leap of faith and ideologically driven mental blocks convinced these very same imbecilic policy-makers to think that it would be a good idea to trade freely with the ultimate mother of all monopolies.

The Chinese Communist Party system and all its arms.

Communist China is really the ultimate form of monopolistic trade counterparty. This is embedded in their legal system and in the legal system of all communist countries that have ever existed.

It is not just the huge Chinese state-owned enterprises and the government that are the problem. It is worse than that.

As has been described by respected publications such as the Financial Times and the Harvard Business Review, and in the recent book "The Party: The Secret World of China's Communist Rulers", every *private* company of any meaningful size in China is also legally obliged to have a Communist Party Cell inside its structure. This cell generally calls the shots in the organization (mainly because they can actually get people "shot" if need be) and coordinates with all the other Party cells in the country, be they competitors, suppliers, provincial and city governments, or the national government.

(Source: https://hbr.org/2014/03/why-china-cant-innovate; http://www.lexology.com/library/detail.aspx?g=9e11432b-fd7b-4239-ade8-0f8f8dc2d9e0; http://chinalawandpolicy.com/tag/ccp/; http://www.economist.com/node/21543575)

If your company has at least 100 employees, according to the law you must have a party cell. It is "recommended" for companies above 50 employees (you feel no pressure here coming from a despotic government, huh?) or where at least three employees are members of the Communist Party of China. Now whether it is 100 or 200 employees, or 500, will change over time. However, that is not the main point. More concerning is that this is even true of almost all subsidiaries of foreign companies as well! No wonder so much technology and trade secrets are stolen!

Think about it.

Compared to this, GM, Ford and Fiat Chrysler meeting to fleece consumers by coordinating prices in full, televised view of everyone in the middle of the Yankees Stadium is peanuts!

Now, the system of Communist Party cells in China, and how they bind together all organizations of any meaningful size in the country, is well known by anyone that does even a small amount of business related to China. In fact, they are known by anyone who knows any communist system. Because remember, while Communist China has made some changes to its economic models since the 1970s, their political system has barely changed at all. After all, this has all been done with the objective of strengthening the Communist Party's grip on society.

Now you can see why the media don't like to talk about it, because then they would have to work very hard to explain why we do so much business with them in the first place. This would ultimately be a fruitless exercise as there are no good reasons for it. You can see how everyone that claims to have a "scientific" reason to trade with China likes to evade any debate on the topic. Especially the media.

This is really just the way all communist political and legal systems works. Ask anyone. Remember the movie "The Hunt for Red October"? The first thing the captain had to do to defect was to kill the political officer, i.e. the head of the party cell of the submarine.

Not many people remember this but Mikhail Gorbachev only ruled as President of the Soviet Union in the last year of its existence. This is because no such role had existed before then! The creation of the position, encompassing the authority to rule the country, was a product of his political reforms, and was a major sign of advancement in itself. Before then, this authority was not at all linked to the legal structure of the country itself but was embedded in the Communist Party of the Soviet Union. His job title when he came to power in 1985 was something like "General Secretary of the Central Committee of the Communist Party of the Soviet Union". The power to rule in a communist system comes from the communist party's structure, not from the national legal system.

Communist systems are characterized by a dual legal system in which the communist party is independent and above the rest of society yet connected to all parts of it, even the nominally private ones, via party cells. Despite all the so-called "economic reforms", this is one part of the communist system that has actually been strengthened in the modern communist China of the past 20 years. This should not surprise anyone, as reforms were only undertaken by the party to protect themselves and the system against the threat of collapse, which really looked real in the early 1990s following the fall of the Soviet Union and the Berlin Wall.

However, the bottom line is that this allows communist China, including companies that are nominally "owned" by private individuals, to exert a degree of collusion and coordination between the state, at all levels, and both public and "private" companies, that is impossible to replicate in any pluralistic society. Like ours. Or even a dictatorship that otherwise operates a capitalism-based economic and legal system.

We certainly don't want to copy them. Doing so would destroy free markets and ultimately democracy. Imagine that – the same organization having the upper hand in the state government of Ohio, in Microsoft, in the Sierra Club, in the FBI and in the construction companies that do business in the Midwest.

However, our societies are slowly having to become more like communist China as a defensive mechanism against the predatory kind of trade relationship that this kind of coordination leads to. Think about all the trade protection measures that we are having to impose with increasing frequency on not just China but the rest of the world? And the growing resistance across the world to foreign investment, foreign acquisitions, and more broadly a general sense of unease about anything foreign? How long can we keep it going until we change the very nature of our own way of life?

So, this is not a conspiracy, because a conspiracy would imply something illegal done covertly, like Toyota and GM colluding in prices.

What we are talking about is a well-established, legal obligation of essentially all organizations in China to be part of the Communist Party structure. This is like taxes. Actually, it's more than taxes, which as you can see, if you have some solid people in your company's Communist Party cell, you can sort of feel relaxed about. In fact, not having such a mechanism in place would threaten the existence of the communist system itself. For the party, that's worth shooting a truckload of very good people for.

So there you go, what pretty much everyone that does some business with China or any communist country knows but no one likes to talk about. This is because talking about it reveals the powerlessness of the people that have to try to do business in China.

In fact, it was even cited by the US government as a reason to block acquisitions by Huawei, a telecom equipment manufacturer from China (http://blogs. ft.com/beyond-brics/2012/11/09/china-party-cells-aid-capitalism/). This is kind of hypocritical if you think about it, considering that Lenovo, also a large Chinese company and undoubtedly subject to the same control mechanisms from the CCP, has been allowed to do much more in the US. Really, people just don't like to talk about it in public.

Unfortunately, considering the significant power of China over the global economy today, both our financial system and the media have to live under this kind of undeclared self-censorship when it comes to issues related to the country. In this sense, the world economy is not unlike a drug lord-dominated poor neighbourhood. No one likes to talk about it, because if you do, they will come for you. You will be unable to continue business as usual. You will lose money, will have to leave in a hurry, and your friends will be afraid of being seen with you in public.

But, you know, just more socially acceptable...

The Chinese government is, in fact, known to retaliate against any foreign organization that says anything that makes it look bad. This happens all the time, even to companies that need to maintain their credibility to continue to prosper, like the Financial Times, the Economist and Bloomberg News (http://www.nytimes.com/2014/03/21/business/international/bloomberg-should-have-rethought-articles-on-china-chairman-says.html?_r=0). Just don't ask them to confirm that in public. You know, Crips vs Bloods. Open your mouth and get whacked. Same thing. Just so China doesn't get the idea to block their Chinese revenues altogether. As Pablo Escobar used to say, "money or lead".

Indeed, to anyone that does even a moderate amount of business relating to China, the Chinese Communist Party is well known for leveraging its significant control and coordination of the entire economic and political system to extract unfair advantages. There are well-known cases in train manufacturing where the Chinese government has poached technology from foreign competitors, with related Chinese companies then using the very same technology to compete internationally at cut-price rates. Foreign companies have also been singled out for "anti-trust" (the irony) breaches of regulation, such as the recent cases in the auto and pharmaceutical sectors (https://hbr.org/2010/12/china-vs-the-world-whose-technology-is-it) (https://www.bloomberg.com/view/articles/2016-05-16/china-s-self-defeating-clampdown-on-multinationals).

Or think about Microsoft, which recently had to leave China entirely after years of being discriminated against by both the country's private and public sectors.

The widespread hacking of foreign companies, many of whom refrain from protesting for fear of retaliation against their business interests in China, has been rightly called by the former head of the US National Security Agency as the "the greatest transfer of wealth in history" (http://www.insidesources.com/ex-nsa-head-chinese-hacking-is-the-greatest-transfer-of-wealth-in-history/).

Yet, as in the case of other sectors with significant monopoly power, there is little that foreign companies in China can do. Even giants such as Microsoft, Bloomberg and Hitachi cannot do much against an organized system of Communist Party cells that permeates the entire country. It ends up just like you and me when we try to deal with a monopoly. We are forced to put up with it.

Yes, even the companies that choose to deal with China will probably lose in the medium to long term. But that's not the point. The point is about cornering the decision makers, right? CEOs of large corporations are not stupid. And they are not evil. But they know that if they try to fight this unfair racket, they will get discriminated against in China, then blocked, then their shareholders will ask questions, then they will get fired, and then they will get replaced by someone else that will do exactly the same thing he refused to do out of principle and good judgement.

This is how the real world works – not through charity, but through incentives. A large monopoly changes your incentives. You hate having to deal with them and yet you have no choice. Not as the system is set up. No matter how powerful someone is, if she doesn't dance to the tune of the universe, she is thrown out and replaced.

Some of them might try to push for some support from our governments, which is unlikely to be effective because our political and economic systems were built on the bases of competition and pluralism, which contains necessary self-regulation mechanisms to avoid collusion and coordination between meaningful parts of those systems. However, it is a system that can easily be played by a single-party state of more than one billion people, as you can imagine.

When it comes to monopoly power and coordination, this is the one game where communist countries excel against capitalist ones. It is therefore not surprising that the natural reaction of the Communist Party in China to the apparent collapse of the communist system in the late 1980s was to create an economic system – let's call it "export-oriented communism" – that would leverage this kind of predatory trade practice that only a communist state would be able to organize.

They rightly realized that the only way that they could continue to finance and maintain the massive inefficiencies of the communist system of planning and coordination was to make the population of other countries, rather than their own population, cover the massive destruction of value inherent to all communist systems. It also meant that they had enough left over to keep their population happy so they wouldn't have to shoot so many of them every day. We will come back to that later.

This wasn't such a big problem when Communist China was small, but it is now dominant in many markets

The more China grows, the more difficult it becomes to avoid being part of this extortion racket.

China is therefore a coordinated monopolist where pretty much all parts of the society work in collusion. However, that did not have that much of an impact on our daily lives as long as China was a tiny economy. Things have changed. Let me show you something:

FIGURE 17 - CHINA'S SHARE OF THE GLOBAL DEMAND FOR KEY COMMODITIES

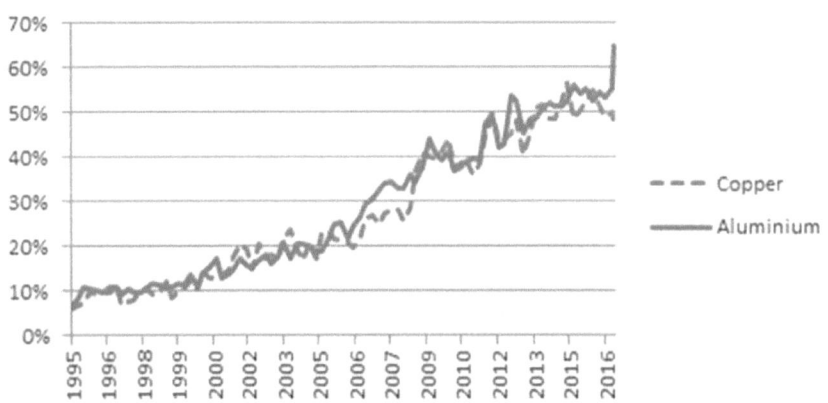

(Source: Author, elaboration of Bloomberg data)

FIGURE 18 - CHINA'S SHARE OF GLOBAL PRODUCTION FOR KEY COMMODITIES

2014

Crude steel production
World total: 1,665 million tonnes

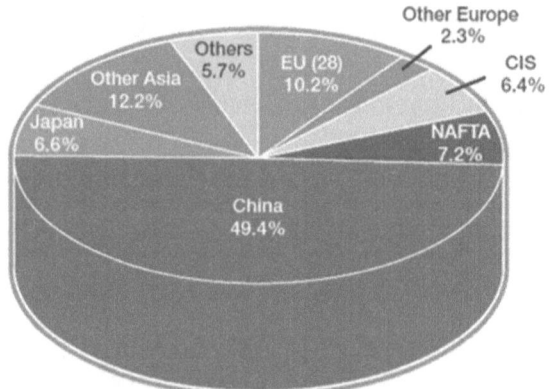

2004

Crude steel production
World total: 1,064 million tonnes

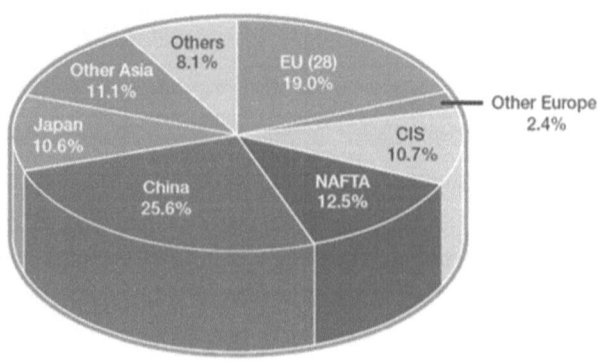

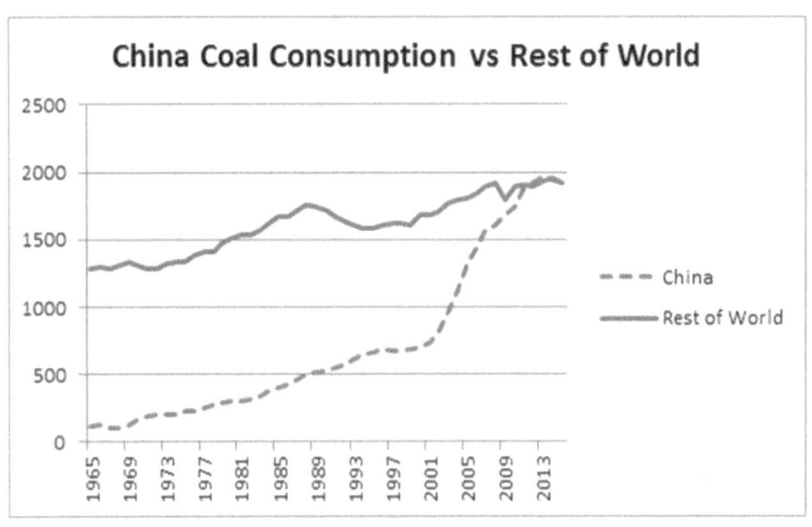

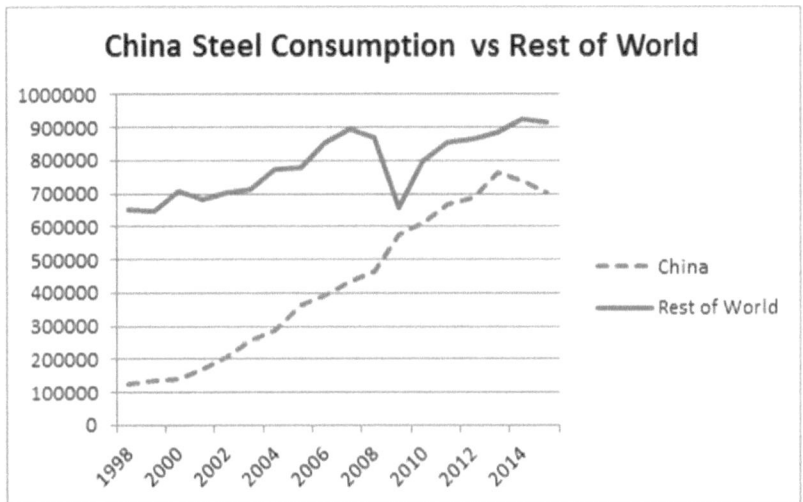

(Source: World Steel Association, World Steel in Figures 2015; from Bloomberg data (million metric tons))

Now, you might be tempted to compare this with the share of the US, or Japan, or even India. However, even on those terms, China is still the big dog.

But as we discussed, that would completely miss the point.

Because the point is that if Ford and GM ever get caught trying to plan their steel purchasing decisions for the next year, it's jail time for everyone. Or

Toyota and Honda. And if the State of Michigan tries to tell Fiat Chrysler what to do, there is a good chance that the company won't listen.

But in China, the entire state as well as both state-owned and private enterprises – let's call it "private" just once for the sake of entertainment value – operate as part of a single command structure. It can torture and accuse you of corruption and put you on live TV to confess your crimes, if you ever have the idea of ignoring its commands. Just like the American CEO of a multinational corporation being extorted out of his technology and profits in China, you have no choice.

So, don't think of the share of the US in that pie, or NAFTA, which is already much smaller than China, as a counterbalance. Split the share of the US into at least 60 pieces and then you will start to have an idea.

OK, so this kind of presence is already enough to have a dominant influence in most of the key markets in the world. Remember, these are the markets that affect your everyday life. Supply and demand. If China decides to build a bridge to nowhere to appease some local communist army chief, steel and copper become more expensive. The expansion of your house that you were planning therefore also becomes much more expensive. Oil prices go up. You need to trade down that truck for a Ford Fiesta. If your country or state specializes in making things instead of borrowing to consume them, i.e. if you are most of Western Europe, Japan, the American Midwest, you are in trouble, because your raw material costs just went up and the people that you sell to are making less money.

FIGURE 19 - OIL PRICES OVER 25 YEARS

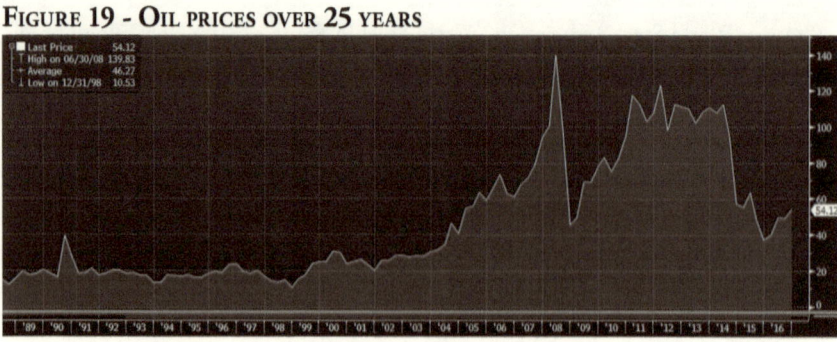

(Source: Bloomberg)

FIGURE 20 – STEEL PRICES OVER 30 YEARS

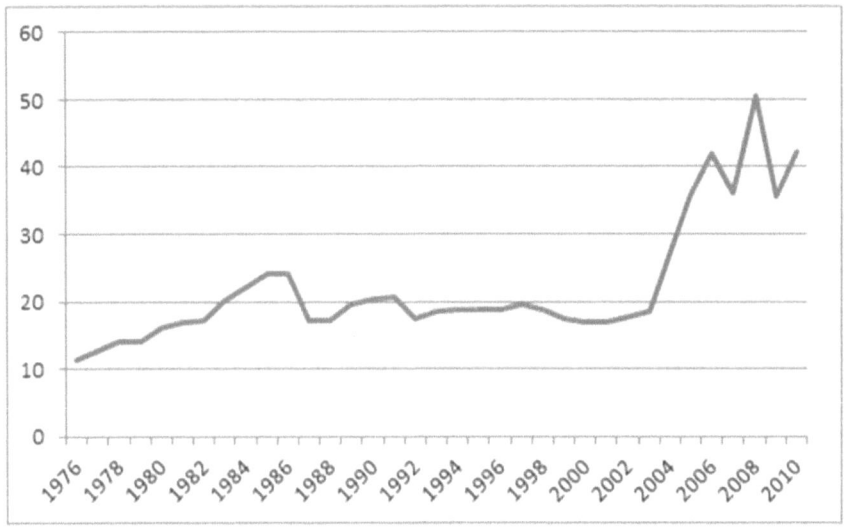

(Source: USGS)

FIGURE 21 - COPPER PRICES OVER 30 YEARS

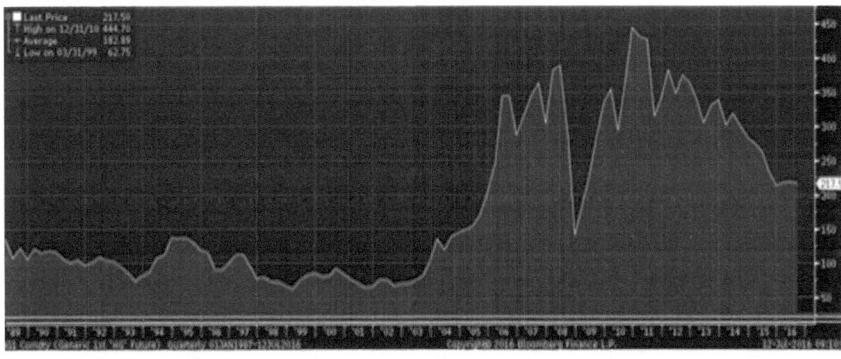

(Source: Bloomberg)

So, as you can see, supply and demand. If the prices of mineral and agricultural products rise, it benefits some people. But not the vast majority of the population of developed countries.

Even if you are one of the few countries that initially benefit, like if you manufacture a lot of mining and construction equipment (like Germany) or you export a lot of minerals and agricultural products (like most of Latin America), you get hit on the way back down. Because what happens is that a communist system of planning is effectively dictating the direction of your economy and entire society via their influence in the global trade.

FIGURE 22 - COMMODITY VERSUS MANUFACTURING EXPORTS AS A % OF TOTAL IN LATIN AMERICA

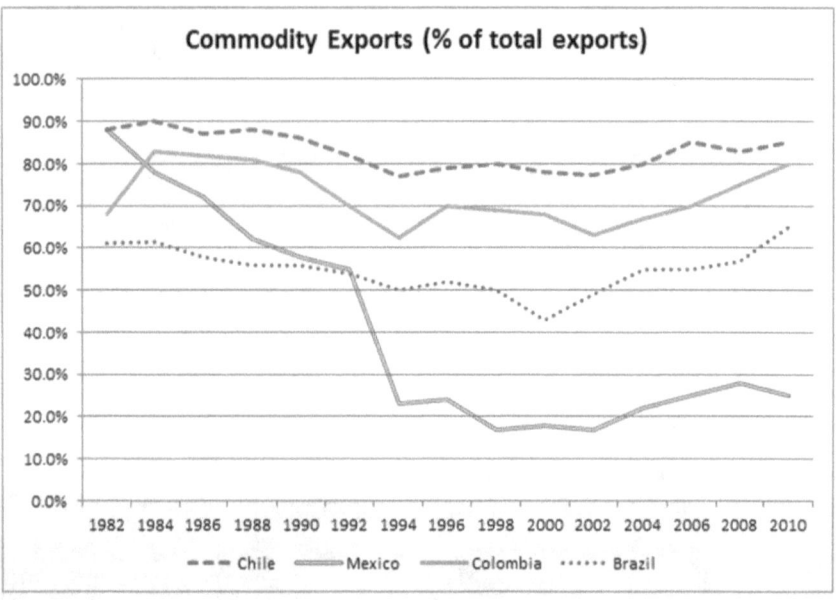

(Source: Author aggregation of international trade statistics)

So Latin America went from having a flourishing manufacturing export-oriented sector in the mid/late 90s to going back 100 years in their economic profile during the past decade to where they were under the colonial system. This is because their economic destiny is almost completely dependent on where the price of coffee, copper or iron ore is. The growing presence of Communist China in the global trading system, with all their dirty tricks, crushed the export competitiveness of these countries in manufacturing.

As you can see from the recent crises in commodity-exporting emerging markets such as Latin America and Africa, pay-back time has already arrived.

Great! So the priorities of the Communist Party of China have become the dominant force in the global economy.

So can we say that communism has become the dominant system for the allocation of scarce resources in the global economy of today?

Now, that's an interesting question.

What liberal economics says, quite rightly, is that the key advantage of capitalism over communism is the market mechanism for the allocation of scarce resources.

Think of two extremes. The entire economy can be planned by some technocrats locked in a room with a lot of calculators and computers, which is more less how it was done in Soviet-style communism. Bridges are built for no good reason. Shops that no one needs are opened and products that no one wants are made. Stuff that everyone needs is in short supply and there are massive lines to buy them. Think of life in the Soviet Union during the Cold War.

Or the economy can follow a natural flow that is the result of millions of people trying to trade for their own benefit. If you see the opportunity of starting a bar in a growing city of the Rockies, you get your savings, maybe borrow some money, and then you do it. This is the same at all levels. Millions of times per year. If you make the right call, you get rewarded. If you make the wrong call, you learn from it and look for another opportunity.

You can see why capitalism beat communism hands down during the Cold War.

Now, in a capitalist system, we all respond to incentives and prices. If you can start a business that makes $10k with $50k of investments, you will do that rather than pay out $100k to make the same amount of money. If the rent of the venue for the bar is too high, maybe you will look for a more affordable location. Or maybe you will try to sell more expensive drinks.

Communism is not like that. If some guys at the top of the Chinese Communist Party decide that Shandong province needs to produce 50m metric tons of steel, they will do it, even if that leads to raw material prices doubling, the maker of the machinery running out of stock and charging them triple, and everything else.

And China is not becoming less communist by any measure. If anything, they are becoming *more* Communist and state-controlled as time passes (http://www.bloomberg.com/gadfly/articles/2016-06-15/comrade-msci-you-need-some-socialist-re-education). What we have seen over the past five years, in areas as diverse as the stock market and investments, is a meaningful increase in state intervention by the Chinese Communist Party.

FIGURE 23 - PUBLIC VERSUS "PRIVATE" INVESTMENTS IN CHINA

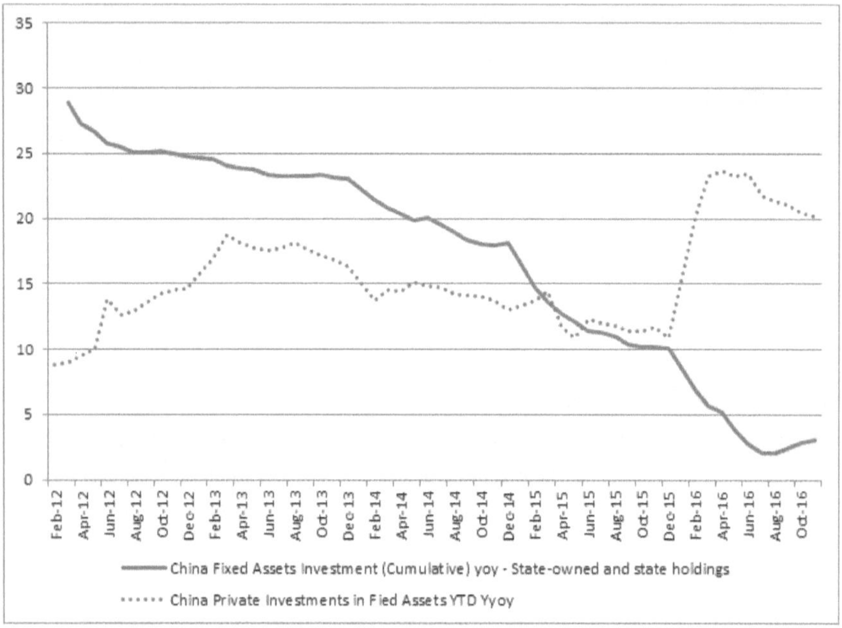

(Source: Author from Chinese statistical data)

Over time, if you have a system that allocates resources effectively and rationally, like capitalism, you should be way ahead of one that tries to do everything for the figurative, ideological and military value of the action at hand.

But if the dominant actor of the global trading system essentially follows communist logic, can you still say that the global economy as a whole still operates as a purely capitalist system?

Think about the Soviet Union. All their decisions only impacted themselves and the other communist countries in their trading block. This is because trade with the capitalist world was very limited and restricted. So if they made a dumb decision to build steel mills that no one needed, or more battle tanks than they could count, their own population suffered. But those outside the communist world were not heavily impacted. Your house still cost the same. Your car still cost the same. Your own steel mill on this side of the world would still go up or down based on the normal dynamics that you would expect in a capitalist economy – supply, demand, competition, technology, innovation, labour relations, proximity to raw materials, and everything else.

This is how the capitalist trading system developed and prospered for several decades while becoming increasingly open. Once more, I emphasize: trade on its own does not lead to declining living standards, as long as it is done with mostly other capitalist countries.

Now, you can see how Chinese Communism having free access to the global trading system has completely changed the picture. Because now, the guys who decide how many bridges get built are the ones in the Communist Party of China. Everyone else has to guess what kind of impact this will have on prices of all tradeable things in the entire world, and try to adapt (survive?) the best they can while trying to turn a profit. Maybe your local bridge will still be repaired? Or maybe not. If you are the guy that repairs bridges, you are out of a job. Not because you are inefficient, or not innovative enough, but simply because a bunch of communist crazies in a room decided that bridges were good and shoes were bad. At least this year.

So you have at best a hybrid system. Outside of China, you still have people mostly trying to do business as usual, although under severe pressure from all of this communist irrationality. But most of the decisions in the capitalist part of the world are heavily influenced by what the Chinese Communist Party does and thinks. This is because their actions have a heavy influence on the price of everything, and in capitalism people make decisions depending on how the prices of some things compare with the price of others. Wages. Fruit. Cars. Housing. Investments. Stocks. Bonds. Retirement. Spending. Saving.

As we have discussed, this is the logical and inevitable impact of having one dominant guy in the market for anything in a capitalist system. No one is meeting in dark corners to conspire to take over the world. It is just that the free market has been subverted by a dominant player. Like the old monopolies of Standard Oil and AT&T but much, much darker – and more powerful.

So communism has become the dominant system for the allocation of scarce resources in the global economy. Especially investment decisions.

This is what I would call a "McDonalds in Pushkin Square" global economy. In the dying days of the Soviet Union, the local communist party, as a sign of reform and openness, decided to allow McDonalds to open a restaurant in Pushkin Square in Moscow. The restaurant was run like any other McDonalds in the world. But all around it, the environment was still determined by the people in the Soviet State Planning Committee (Gosplan).

And this is how these false "liberals" misrepresented the established theory of economics to justify free trade with a large Communist country controlled by a violent and brutal Communist Party.

As you can see around you, this is killing capitalism. This is draining the wages of the middle class and the poor in developed countries. This is distorting the entire global economy via the change in the relative price of everything against everything. This is leading to investments and capital flowing to the people who are the least efficient in using them, destroying massive amounts of wealth per year.

And we are already getting to a breaking point; to a point where the misrepresentation of liberal economic theory as a "scientific" justification of this madness (while true liberal economics actually says the opposite) has led to a backlash against free trade and capitalism in general, against many of the good principles of trade and rational regulation, and many of the things that have been beneficial to us over the post-WWII period.

Even basic pillars of our societies, such as tolerance and respect for diversity of opinion, which we have learned to take for granted since the end of the colonial empires and the Civil Rights movement in the US, are now under increasing strain. We now live in societies where political violence and polarization are going back to levels not seen since the 1960s.

And there goes the last "argument" of these misrepresenting imbeciles. Trading with China is clearly not leading to a gradual opening of the communist system and their convergence towards capitalism and democracy, as these overconfident fools, fresh from a Cold War with a lesser form of communist competition, were led to believe when they admitted China to the World Trade Organization in the early 2000s.

It is instead our societies and economies that are gradually converging more and more to the way the Chinese Communist Party has always operated.

But trade with Communist China is not a zero sum game... It's actually a NEGATIVE sum game.

Now, the false "liberals" whose ideology unwillingly (or maybe in some cases willingly) stands for supporting the worst enemy of global capitalism will tell you that trade with China is not a zero sum game.

What they mean is that when there is trade as a result of competition, specialization and mutual exchange, the system as a whole – i.e. the sum of the welfare of both trading counterparties – is supposed to be better off.

But remember that these silly people are guilty of the very basic logical atrocity of trying to use a model of free competition to justify trade with a Communist entity.

Now from what we have seen, I guess we must agree with them…

It is not a zero sum game.

It is a negative sum game.

What they mean by trade "not being a zero sum" game, but a positive sum game, is this. As we have seen before.

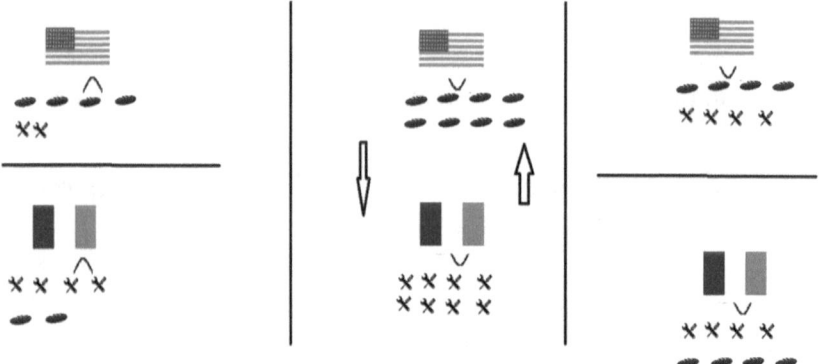

In this way, both sides are better off, and the distribution of the benefits is more or less proportional. This is France trading with the US, so countries with relatively similar standards of living, hence the massive pressure on wages on one of the sides is not big enough to be meaningful. It could be Germany. Or Japan. Or the UK. Or Italy. Or Spain.

And to be fair to these poor fools, as we discussed, they were right most of the time during the history of mankind, at least before China became a meaningful part of the global trading system. This is because major trading countries would either be capitalist - in which case there would be a decent overall benefit from trading - or would be a communist country locked out of the global trading system, in which case they would do very economically destructive things but the only people paying for it were their own. This is represented by a chart of perfect competition supply and demand.

FIGURE 26 - PERFECT COMPETITION MODEL

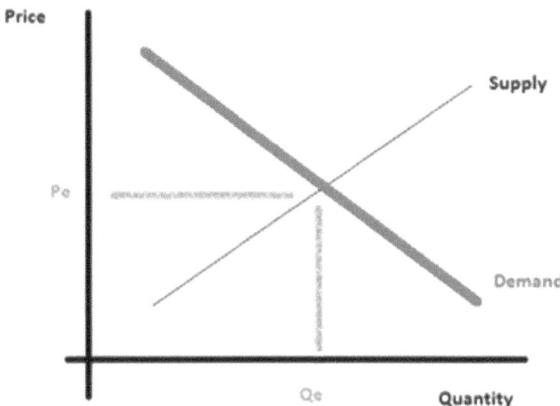

(Source: <u>Author</u>)

So this is certainly a system with a positive sum. For most of the history of economics, liberal trade theory was crucial to defend free trade when the benefits were overwhelming and the difference in standards of living were not that big. All you had to do was to convince both societies that the spoilers who were trying to block this trade from happening (like, for instance, the inefficient guy that originally produced tools in the US above) should step aside in the interest of both societies and the world.

Now below is how a country that has the ability to manipulate its own exchange rate, block access to its market, force any company that wants to sell to them to open a factory in the country, unfairly subsidise sectors that they favour for some arcane reason, and so on, would trade. This is an abstract representation of what is happening when a capitalist country decides to engage with China for trade, trade here being a general term that includes investments, technological exchanges, and everything else.

FIGURE 27 - HOW TRADE WITH COMMUNIST CHINA INSTEAD LOOKS (CHINA HAS
THE LION'S SHARE OF THE BENEFITS)

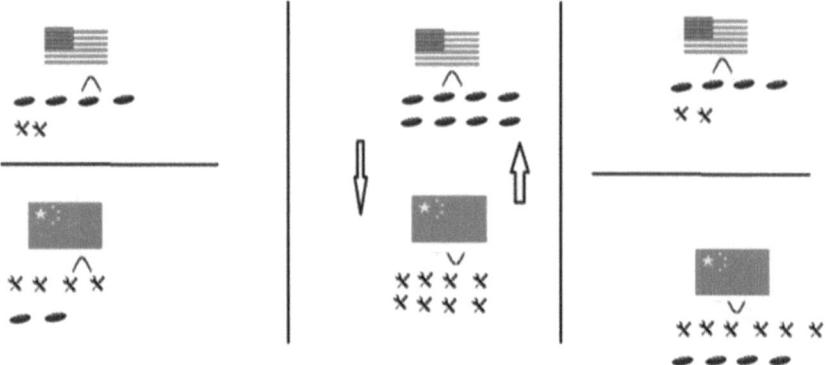

As we can see, trade is happening. But one side is taking almost all of the benefits. And if you include the impact of the lower wages on the side of the richer country (the US), then you can see how almost the entire population of the US is losing from this relationship. They were better off without it. Which we intuitively know today just by looking around us. Refer to our previous chart on stagnant household incomes.

Of course, what enables a large communist trading entity to manipulate the trade in order to skew it to itself is the same thing that allowed our old and new monopolies, like Standard Oil, AT&T and Microsoft, to do the same. It is the monopoly power. Something that the false "liberals" conveniently papered over even as they discuss on a daily basis the importance of having effective anti-trust regulation in their own societies.

FIGURE 28 - TECHNICAL REPRESENTATION OF TRADE WITH A MONOPOLIST

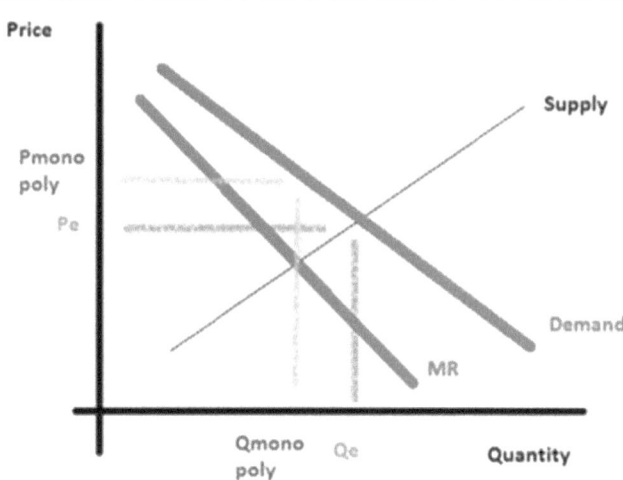

(Source: Author)

So you can see how foolish it is to say that trade is "not a zero-sum game" for anyone who is on the capitalist side of the trade. Just on the basis of this alone, it would be a "negative sum game" in practical terms. But wait. It gets worse.

Now because the US is trading more with China, other countries are losing their market share of the US trade. France can't sell that much hardware in the US anymore. The monopolist is therefore also dislocating the free market competitor.

For several decades after WWII, the capitalist global trading system prospered because the growing and significant benefits of increasingly free trade were reinvested by the most advanced nations of the world, mostly into themselves, generally in an economically rational, capitalist manner. This means following the normal market mechanisms that we discussed in terms of prices, rates of return, optimization of capital needs, and so on.

Now we have a situation in which the surplus of the system is increasingly redirected to a country that, effectively, still operates mostly as a communist entity.

It has been proven over and over again in history that communist systems are horrible managers of scarce resources, especially savings and capital. It has been once again proven over the past ten years in China – a period in which the country went on a massive borrowing and investment binge to build mostly wasteful infrastructure, such as empty ghost towns, steel plants that no one needs, and so on. And never mind what the proponents of the "China point of view" might say, people who works in financial markets and commodities industries know there is no real evidence of any change of heart on this. (See for instance - http://www.forbes.com/sites/kenrapoza/2015/07/20/what-will-become-of-chinas-ghost-cities/#45073991751b, http://www.theguardian.com/world/2016/jan/22/chinese-steel-production-abandoned-mills-broken-lives).

It is increasingly the mainstream view, even in financial circles, that China is having a very distortive impact on global trade. As the US Treasury Secretary Jack Lew recently put it, "excess capacity is distorting markets and important global commodities".

(http://www.bloomberg.com/news/articles/2016-06-03/lew-says-china-s-overcapacity-skewing-markets-u-s-to-push-cuts).

This is not really surprising to anyone who is old enough to remember the suicidal inefficiency of Soviet Communism – a system that led to generalized poverty in a large number of otherwise extremely advanced societies, such as Russia, Hungary and Poland. Communism is one of the most inefficient systems ever devised for peacetime.

Now consider what happens when you have a parasitic communist trading entity freely trading with the rest of the world.

China "trades" with rest of the world

1

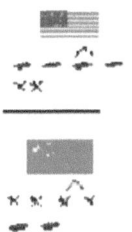
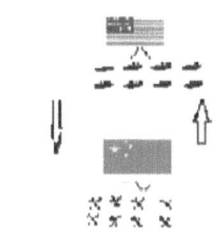
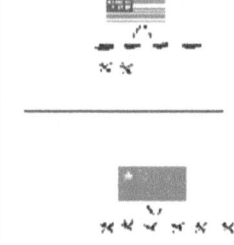

China destroys massive amounts of wealth Communist-style

2

3 China can only prevent its Communist system from collapsing by extracting wealth from other countries

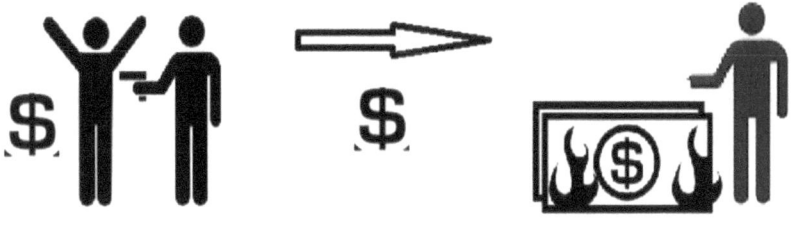

Now we see why this is a genuine "negative-sum" trading system.

The wealth that was before re-circulated and reinvested in a more or less rational way around highly efficient countries is now being mostly channelled into a Communist black hole from which it will never emerge.

FIGURE 30 - US TRADE DEFICIT WITH CHINA OVER THE PAST 30 YEARS

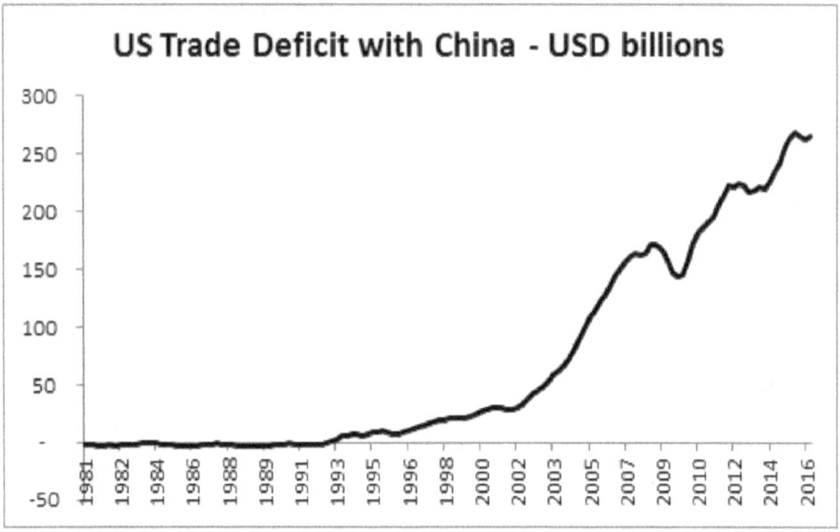

US Trade Deficit with China - USD billions

(Source: Author, elaboration of Bloomberg and international statistical data)

In this system, what you have is essentially the capitalist part of the world paying for the mistakes of the Communist Party of China. And the capitalists will continue to pursue this path until this process reaches a limit in which the global economy is too weak to plug this massive hole year after year.

Now, this is essentially the same thing that the Soviet Union did with its own population and the population of the other communist countries at the time. However, they had little ability or preparation to extract wealth from the capitalist part of the world, except perhaps during the oil crises of the 1970s, and thus quickly ran out of world to suck dry. This is because they were mostly locked out of the healthy (capitalist) parts of the global trading system.

Their own economy became too weak to support this madness, so they started to borrow from abroad. In the end, what economists call "external constraints", which means having to borrow from people who you do not control – mostly foreigners - hit a limit and these systems collapsed in on themselves.

Now here is the key difference between Communist China and the Soviet Union. China *is* part of the global trading system. During the Cold War, you could make a movie like Red Dawn with the Soviet Union as a villain. This is because they had little commercial power to influence what was happening in the society and economy of the US at the time. But when they tried to do a new Red Dawn movie a few years ago, they were unable to cast China (the obvious replacement for the Soviet Union) as the villain. China is way too integrated into the global economy for that to fly. China has commercial clout today that the Soviet Union never had.

What the Chinese Communist Party in some way has grasped is that a communist system and power structure is sustainable as long as you make the populations of other countries pay for it, instead of just your own. By solving the one issue that brought all inefficient systems in history to their knees – the "external constraints" – China managed to create some prosperity for themselves at the expense of others.

Now, the problem is that the global economy as a whole is running into "external constraints". Look around you. Growth slowing everywhere. Productivity growth stalling. Financial crises popping up here and there with increasing frequency.

FIGURE 31 - PRODUCTIVITY GROWTH – DEVELOPED VERSUS EMERGING MARKETS
Labour productivity growth[1]

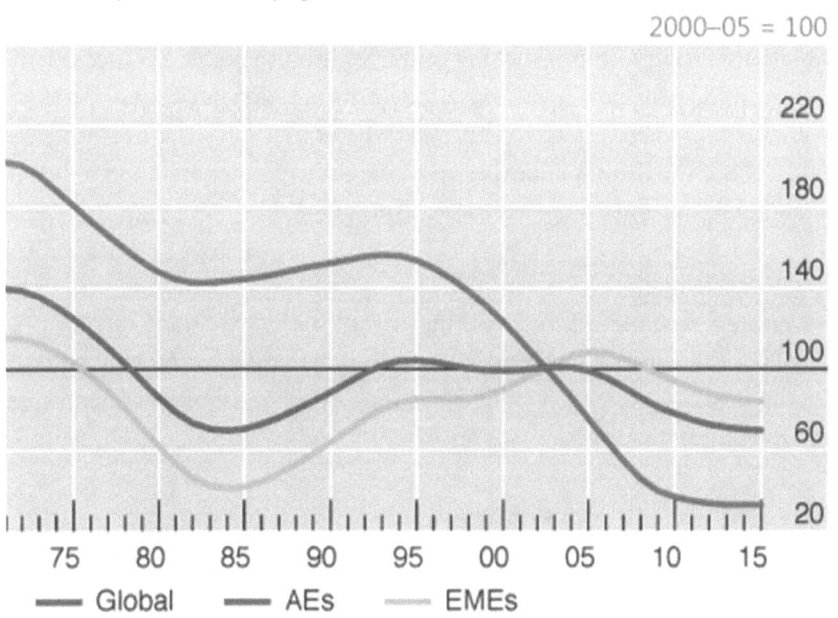

(Source: BIS www.bis.org – note – AEs: advanced economies; EMEs: Emerging Economies).

China used to be a small tick sucking the blood from the back of the global trading system. Now this tick has grown to the size of a Harley Davidson. The host, which is the rest of the global economy, is weakened, pallid, and stumbling. We can see the natural limit of the process approaching rapidly. Yet the tick will not stop sucking until both it and the host are dead. Because that's just how international parasitic relationships have worked in human history.

What killed the Soviet Union – an incredibly inefficient economic and political system sucking the blood of an increasingly weakened real economy – is what is killing the global economy today.

We are being killed by communism. Yes, in the 21st century. After Gorbachev and Deng Xiaoping, Ronald Reagan and Pokémon. After communism was supposed to be ancient history on a par with the 10 plagues of Egypt.

This trade is a "negative sum game" as you can see. The massive destruction of wealth by the Communist Party and all its parts in the public and "private" sector of China only exists because trade with the capitalist world has plugged the hole of wealth destruction inherent to communist systems.

Because this relationship is sucking resources from the most advanced parts of the world, you have less innovation in production processes. Or even in products. You have less wealth everywhere. You have the death of the middle class. The rise of political extremism. Growing economic and political instability. Houses are more expensive. And so on.

Now we have one of the most inefficient systems of allocation of resources ever created – communism – making the allocation decisions for most of the global economy. Why are people still wondering why economic growth is going down all over the world? Have they never heard of what happened with the Soviet Union?

So the commies have won this round.

They beat the overconfident "post-Soviet collapse" developed countries at their own game. They proved how an export-oriented communist country, by leveraging the high degree of internal coordination that only a communist regime has, can turn the rest of the global trading system into a softer version of the colonies of the early 1900s.

In a way, it is natural that the Chinese Communist Party decided that these predatory/parasitic trading practices would be the way out of the scare they had at the massacre in Tiananmen Square and the fall of Soviet communism. Communism is not good at innovation, competition and freedom of choice. It cannot win against capitalism in a level playing field. Communism is good at extorting and coercing people, and that's what they have done on a global scale. The Soviet Union showed that doing this only on a domestic scale was not a viable long-term strategy – you have to shoot a lot of people to keep them quiet. One day they will be stronger than you and will come to shoot you, and so your communist party will collapse.

One of the worst "excuses" that I have heard on why it would be good to trade with communist China, even with all of these obvious risks, is that over time, trading openly with communist China would convince the country to become more open, capitalistic and democratic and ultimately be "converted" into the Western form of democracy and free market capitalism. This must be one of the dumbest mainstream ideas ever advanced in the history of mankind, and trust me, it is not short on competition. It is probably up there with the ideas of burning people at the stake for suspected witchcraft, with no less dire consequences.

As we have discussed here, it is logical and common sense that the current trading dynamics that the rest of the world has with China would not lead to the Chinese Communist Party "converging" with liberal democracy. Quite the opposite! As you can see, the longer this dynamic goes on, the longer political and economic extremism will flourish in our societies. The longer a growing number of people in our societies will be calling for a strongman to put things right again. And the longer countries will have to increasingly resort to trade protectionism and a general withdrawal from free trade in order to protect their economies. Think about what has been happening in the global market of solar panels and steel recently, where China's dumping has led to a general increase in trade barriers the world over!

Fortunately, the advanced societies of the world did not survive 3,000 years of unforgiving Darwinist competition without developing defence mechanisms that kick in in times of crises such as this. We are already seeing a growing awareness of the situation, despite the fact that the general "scientific" economic debate is still dominated by this misrepresentation of economic "liberalism".

As I mentioned, this dynamic is reaching the limits of how long it can go, just like the Soviet Union in the early 1990s, but on a global scale. We are already seeing signs around us, both economic and political, that we are very close to breaking point.

We have moved from a period when global trade was both economically beneficial and generally popular – the 1945-1990 period – to much darker times. A time when open trade is increasingly becoming the main political battleground in our societies. A time when hard choices are being made for us when we try to duck the responsibility and dignity of making them ourselves.

There is no secret to what was effectively missing from the global trading system back in 1945-1990, but what we now have hanging like a sword over everything that we have built.

Communism.

Communist China.

So now we are reaching a T-junction where either the solution will be found in a relatively organized, rational manner that preserves the advancements that we have made in the social, political and economic arena. Or it will be a violent backlash that will throw away the good – trade with other countries of similar income levels, political tolerance, racial tolerance, and so on – with the bad – China trade.

It is natural for Darwinist systems such as human societies to oscillate between two extremes and never reach equilibrium, like a pendulum. In a Darwinist system, a system-wide reaction is always triggered by a process that cannot be indefinitely sustained, such as communism in general and trade with Communist China in particular. So I believe it is extremely likely that the process described above will come to a sudden halt in the near future.

But T-junctions can go many ways. Compare Imperial Japan with Franco's Spain, the British Raj, Communist Russia and early 1900s USA. A society can react to a major change in the global context by coming together after a relatively brief period of internal conflict, like Imperial Japan did. Or it can fall into a situation of sharp, extreme polarization and ultimately a long and brutal civil war, leading back to a relatively rational and brutal system, as in Franco's Spain. Or that civil war can lead to an even worse outcome, such as a permanent shift towards an isolationist, inefficient and totalitarian regime such as the Soviet Union, and endure for a long time.

Societies can also react by disintegrating in the face of an external threat, with each part ultimately being thrown against each other by internal as well as external dynamics, such as India during the period of British rule. Finally, a society can react by evolving its economic and political system in a relatively organized way that benefits all in that society, such as the USA of the early 1900s.

The outcomes of Darwinist systems, though obvious and inevitable with the benefit of hindsight (feudalism, renaissance, industrialization), are often very difficult if not impossible to predict in advance – especially for those that are part of it, like ourselves. Consider the complexity of the system as well as the fact that all observers, including us, are inevitably influenced and biased by the information that is closest to us and to our heart.

This is a lesson that Communists should have learned, with their "scientific" view of the evolution of history and economics from the perspective of the "class struggle". We can say that this is a relatively naïve view, again with the benefit of hindsight, considering that the different components of a society have historically done far better by pillaging other societies (European colonial powers, today's communist China) than by pillaging each other (Soviet Union, the French revolution, the old communist China). But this is a powerful view nonetheless, especially from the perspective of the European working classes during the mid-1800s.

Now I will try to put forward what I think is most likely to happen, if we do not address this problem, based on my knowledge of how human societies have reacted to challenges of such magnitude previously.

THE DANGER

There is a risk of a Soviet-style breakdown of the global trading system, initiated by one or more of the most important developed countries

In economics, history and nature, coordinated and rational solutions are often prescribed but almost never occur. There are very strong reasons for that. In almost every situation, the different components of a society will seek to adopt the conservative approach to fence their own garden and minimize loss to their own turf, as opposed to pursuing lofty "give and take" solutions that are best for the system as a whole.

This is also known as Darwinism. A "solution" is always found. But the "solution" is the sum of the forces of all of the elements in a system, as opposed to a planned course of action. History does not determine who is right. History determines who is left.

The first thing we can expect to occur with a fairly high degree of confidence is the end of the current system as it is. In history, economic systems that are perceived as having failed to deliver results over a relatively long period of time, let's say two or three decades, have almost always met a certain end, usually at the hands of their own people. And if we look around us, we can see growing signs of generalized unhappiness with the economic system as it is currently set up. Right and left. Black and white. Middle class and poor, and even the rich. Extremist parties are rising on both sides and the "centre" ground quickly disappearing.

So a "solution" will be found, just as a Darwinist system finds a "solution" to all systems that are inherently out of balance. It is not a solution from some good people going into a room and compromising on a rational goal. It is the sum of the individual reactions of all participants in a society, and of all societies relative to one another. It can be violent. It can create more problems than it solves. But generally it will go in the direction of taking care of the key issues currently affecting the global economy. One way or another. Sooner or later.

Unfortunately, I think it is highly likely that the world will continue to trend towards higher barriers to trade, in terms of tariffs, non-tariff barriers, exchange rate manipulation, or everything else that the ingenuity of the human mind is able to devise.

Because of the nature of the global trading system, meaningful change is unlikely to occur until a relatively large trading bloc, such as the United States or European Union, takes the lead in explicitly breaking away from the ongoing "soft" trade war towards a more explicit one. The US is a more formalized political entity – I would not dare say more cohesive. But the European Union is currently facing a growing crisis of legitimacy, as illustrated by the recent Brexit vote in the UK. And they may face a threat to their own existence if they don't renounce their heavily ideological, "good for post-war but bad for today's world" commitment to relatively free trade with countries such as communist China.

However, even the Communist Chinese "model of growth" is now beginning to meet external constraints. Export-oriented Chinese Communism is just getting too big to continue the parasitic trading policies that worked so well when China was a much smaller economy. So I would not discard the possibility that the breakdown could actually happen within China itself. While the EU is generally very divided, I can see the momentum already building in all of the key countries of the region, which is amazing considering how differently each of them has been impacted by the trends discussed. My money would be on the US starting the process, though, as it has more cohesive and centralized national leadership.

Unfortunately, when that happens, I suspect that we are at least as likely to see an all-against-all kind of trade war, similar to what we saw after the 1929 crisis, instead of a coordinated response that would seek to preserve the good aspects of the existing global trade system. These benefits, again, are mainly trade with the non-communist countries, and trade between developed countries, or even some of the trade between developed and developing countries.

This outcome would mean pretty much what we had in the 1930s, which ultimately led to WWII. Each country closes themselves in on their own mini trade zone. Then they create a large number of tariff and non-tariff barriers to keep companies from other countries away. When you cannot trade with another country, military invasions are the only way to capture its market. War becomes profitable. And we human beings like to go after profits.

That is usually bad for everyone. But considering the damage that trading with communist China has done to all large developed economies, it will probably feel much better than the current situation for the vast majority of the population of the developed countries.

I suspect that we don't need a clear break from the old political order in order for this outcome to take place. It is almost as likely to be initiated by someone like Mikhail Gorbachev, an insider who is put in power in the hopes of trying to save the current system, but is instead gradually and somewhat reluctantly forced to yield to the immense pressure of reality.

The key motivation for a leader of the US, or a leader of the key European Union countries, to push for such change could be similar to what the leaders of the old Soviet Union faced – a generalized unhappiness with the system and a threat to the continued existence of the country as it is, as these economic factors naturally affect some regions more than others, some races more than others, and bear down especially heavy on the middle class. One could argue that these systems are more likely to break down into many district countries than action be taken, but the history of the 1900s would suggest to me that they are more likely to circle the wagons and a solution evolve that closes down the system for the sake of preserving it.

It is also quite possible that the key motivation will simply be the easy pickings of the huge immediate benefits to be derived from ending the trade with communist China, which will at one point begin to look more tempting than the more comfortable but increasingly unsustainable current path.

There is also a very high risk of us seeing free market capitalism discredited together with the unrealistic trade theories of the false "liberals". This would be a pity, as it would destroy many of the good things we learned to take for granted over the past 40 years. Like an efficient stock market. Or a general reduction in the role of the government in productive sectors. Yet, the misrepresented "liberal" economic "argument" has been that you could not have all these without having the imbecilic trade with communist China thrown in too, which is the inverse of the truth. But as leaders scramble for solutions to remain in power and preserve the continued existence of the current political systems, the baby risks being thrown out with the bath water.

So we have two possibilities ahead of us. Either the current global trading system is saved in some form, by getting rid of the parts of it that are leading to a generalized declined in the standards of living of the population of developed countries. Or we could have everyone drawing up their bridges and locking themselves in their own trading zone, which would be very harmful for the economies of these countries, yet lead to better standards of living than the current system, and would be the more natural way in which human societies have reacted in the absence of coordination.

The key determinant of which way we will go is the dynamics of the organizations in which communist China still does not have a major presence. This would probably be the G-7, which is comprised of the United States, Canada, France, Germany, Italy, Japan, and the United Kingdom. During the immediate post-Soviet Union period, the G-7 possessed an unusual amount of economic power. This has been heavily diluted by the rise of communist China. Yet, it remains the only forum of countries that is large enough to command influence, yet small enough to realistically enable a degree of coordination.

This, however, is a big if. The different countries of the G-7 have been affected very differently by the rise of communist China in the global trading system. And as we know, communist China's usual strategy is to use its commanding influence to throw one group against the other. Yet, even in the countries that have historically been most favourable towards continued free trade with China, such as Canada, Germany and the UK, the deep unpopularity of the current trading arrangements among their own populations is already bringing about a change of heart. Think about the recent UK referendum in favour of leaving the European Union, for instance (Brexit). The UK's struggle to save its steel sector in the face of Chinese dumping, the relative stagnation of Ontario's manufacturing sector, and growing German unease with Chinese acquisitions of key technologies in the country (such as robotics) are all clear signs of that. So we will see.

In this context, I will move on to consider the potential ideal "solutions" for the serious crisis that the populations of the developed countries are currently facing. This requires healthy scepticism and humility to recognize that in real-world situations, societies don't search rationally for ideal "solutions" that maximize the benefits for everyone. Instead they oscillate, sometimes violently, between different partial answers until a certain accommodation is found, depending on the relative equilibrium of power and the interests of the key actors inside and outside of the society.

SOLUTION

Labour differential tariffs, isolation of communist China, or all-against-all trade war – which one is better? And which one is most likely to happen?

Once again, we should recognize that the evolution of human history, and the way in which all Darwinist systems oscillate around the balance to an extremely complex set of challenges that seemed impossible to predict at first, should humble us all. For instance, who would have predicted that the poverty and sharp class divisions of the early industrial period would evolve, after much struggle, into the middle class-based societies of today?

In this spirit of exploration and open discussion, let me consider some solutions to our current predicament. I will start from the ideal, which means the ones that would directly address the root causes of the problems we face while seeking to avoid damage to the beneficial parts of the current global trade system. Then I will consider how realistic such solutions could be, and finally propose a more likely and "natural" outcome considering the general way in which societies have historically solved similar issues in the past.

Labour differential tariffs – ideal but vulnerable to being gamed by communist China

As mentioned before, trade between countries at similar stages of economic development tends to be highly beneficial for the vast majority of the population of both countries. Effectively, in such circumstances, trade between France and the US would be generally similar to trade between two French cities or two American states. Both parties gain from the competition, scale and specialization that such trade can provide.

FIGURE 32 - TRADE BETWEEN DEVELOPED COUNTRIES AS AN OVERALL BENEFICIAL, NON-ZERO-SUM RELATIONSHIP.

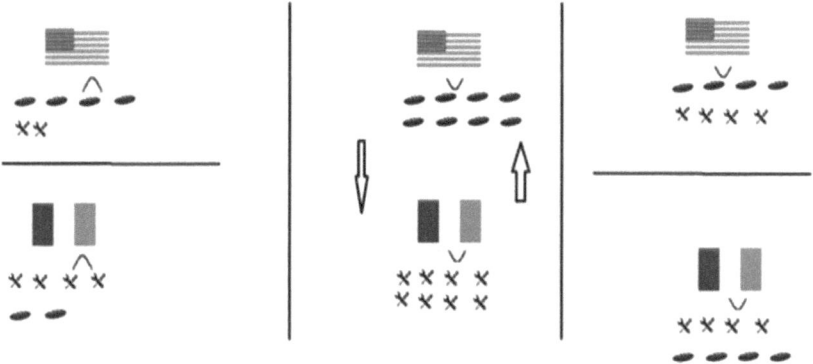

How can we preserve political and social support for this system that has brought us prosperity and relative peace, and protect it from the form of trade that has generally harmed the population of the developed countries over the past 20 years?

One way would be to make sure that the good elements of international trade – competition, freedom of choice, specialization, innovation – are maintained, while minimizing the part that has such harmful effects on the populations of the developed countries (the relative erosion of real wages and the severe dilution of capital per worker).

An import tariff that would be determined specifically by the difference in the level of wages in each trading partner, in my view, would have the direct impact of levelling the playing field for wage costs while maintaining the benefits of international trade. If one country has a wage level that is half another's, then you slap on a tariff to make sure that this wage differential, on its own, will not lead to an unfair competitive advantage for the companies that decide to relocate production out of the richer country.

I would call it a labour differential tariff.

It would have major advantages over a general increase in tariffs (or trade barriers more generally) for all trade partners, rich and poor. This was what was tried in the aftermath of the 1929 crisis, and only led to more crises and ultimately to war. To be honest, this all-against-all trade conflict seems to be what the world has slowly but surely been trending to for 10 years, from currency wars/money printing/quantitative easing to anti-dumping cases, subsidies and protectionist regional trade agreements. Indeed, past historical experience would suggest that it is a common reaction by societies in crisis to eventually blame external parties (which by definition are not represented in such societies) and shut the door on everyone. Good and bad.

A general and indiscriminate increase in trade barriers against everyone would destroy a lot of the trade that is overwhelmingly beneficial to both sides involved - the kind of trade that the simple comparative advantage model is meant to represent. We would not have the parasitic trade from China. But we would also not have the fairly priced and quality cars that were born from the healthy competition between the US, Europe and Japan. Or the affordable quality electronics. Maybe we would be a bit better off than before, considering the overwhelming damage that the China trade is causing, but not that much better.

With the generate corporate drive towards the easy pickings of lower wages taken out of the equation, we would certainly have more competition on other factors. Who has the better management? Who has the most efficient production processes? Who has the best products? Where are the best places to do business? Innovation at all levels would accelerate. The stagnation that has plagued the standards of living of the developed countries over the past 20 years would become a distant memory.

Implementation would also be straightforward, as the general level of wages from country to country are broadly well known. And it could be applied only in the case of a material differential in wages. Obviously, there is not much point in the US putting up such a tariff on Canada just because this year Canadian wages dipped 7-8% below American ones, on the back of exchange rate fluctuations or other fickle factors.

While there are potentially other instruments that could also try to directly address the issue of the relative wage level and capital per worker of each country, most would require some extensive and difficult calculations or negotiations, or could incentivize companies to potentially relocate even more activity outside of developed countries.

We don't want a system like the global taxation system today – a system so complex that it ultimately favours only those that are large enough to be able to afford the vast expenses required to game it.

In this sense, labour differential tariffs would be a simple, objective, hard rule to address the direct harm from trade today. In this sense, it would be less vulnerable to lobbying, begging, whining, and all other forms of pressure from the parties that stand to gain from a breach of the rules, even at the expense of society as a whole.

And, as much as we don't like to use this word very often in economics or financial markets, it would be FAIR.

Now, being fair is not so important – unless you are trying to convince other people to back free market capitalism before it is thrown away Russian communist revolution-style. Then fair is a very good common point of reference.

Our societies spent centuries making incredible sacrifices to transition away from generalized poverty so that our kids could have a better life. The general fabric of our societies, the middle class societies, are predicated on this implicit contract. True, Darwinism can crush unrealistic notions of fairness (like communism). But the notion of fairness can dictate which path a society will ultimately take. And that is Darwinism too. Even more than the balance of supply and demand, much as we like it.

Having said that, I suspect that this would ultimately not fully address the main problem with the global trading system. The elephant in the room. Or the 800-pound gorilla – the Communist Party of China, and its highly coordinated presence in the global economy.

This is because low wages are only the tip of the iceberg of the harm that the presence of this entity in the global trading system is causing us.

While the labour differential tariff would address the issue of low wages, in the absence of action specifically designed to counter the parasitic trading practices of the Chinese Communists, it would also disproportionally impact the countries that have relatively low wages but are otherwise honest traders, like Mexico or Colombia.

Ultimately, because of their large presence in the global trading system, the Chinese communists also have growing power to use the lure of their large market to pit some countries against others. Like the US against the EU. Or the EU against Japan. Or even Germany against France. All of that would severely dilute the efficacy of any remedial measure that would keep them as part of the system. And because of the communist power structure that rules both the public and private sector in China, this is a game that they are ultimately well positioned to win. You can't out game a large, monolithic communist trading entity unless you become one yourself.

The misrepresentation of "liberal" economics became a body of pick-and-choose "scientific" justification on why it is a good idea to trade freely with a large, monolithic communist economy specifically set up to extract capital, demand and technology from us. Good old Adam Smith would be turning in his grave.

This is the problem with those that call themselves the "free trade" people. They want to avoid any mention of how China distorts trade because they fear that an attack on free trade with China is an attack on free trade with everyone else.

But as I am trying to clarify, it's the other way around. Free trade with China *endangers* free trade with everyone else, both internationally and inside each country. Free trade with a large and monolithic communist country is effectively changing the capitalist system into something resembling communism more and more.

Exclude China completely from the global trading system. The global economy cannot return to normality unless this is done.

As much as a labour differential tax would be a good start, it would not be enough.

That is because any specific measures that are directed at preventing the Chinese communists from gaming the global trading system in their favour are likely to be circumvented.

Our societies have evolved as pluralistic societies. This has brought us many advantages. Innovation. Freedom of choice. Competition. But it also leaves us vulnerable to any entity that stitches the entire political and economic system of a country into a formal, highly coordinated structure that is meant by its very design to be impervious to external influence.

Therefore, unfortunately there are no realistic halfway measures that can preserve any benefit that we derive from Chinese trade against the massive harm that it causes us in all its forms.

The only other choice would be to become ourselves a mirror image of what China is today – a country where the interests of the individual are trumped by the grandiose plans of the state. Where diversity of opinion is crushed in the name of internal cohesion. Essentially, that would mean that the communists have won. And we have lost. Because they turned the world communist. Without firing a single shot. Well, maybe a few, here and there, but you get my point.

If you think about it, this is already happening to us, to a certain extent. Large corporations and governments across the developed world are increasingly coordinating their actions in the name of self-defence against the trading practices of communist China. Trade barriers, tariffs but mainly non-tariff barriers, are rising across the world. The growth of global trade is stagnating. And indeed, from a Darwinist perspective, this is exactly what you would expect to happen. Societies adapt or die. The most dominant party can dictate the response of others. Currency wars. Local content rules. Anti-dumping cases.

FIGURE 33 - GROWTH IN INTERNATIONAL TRADE SLOWING DOWN

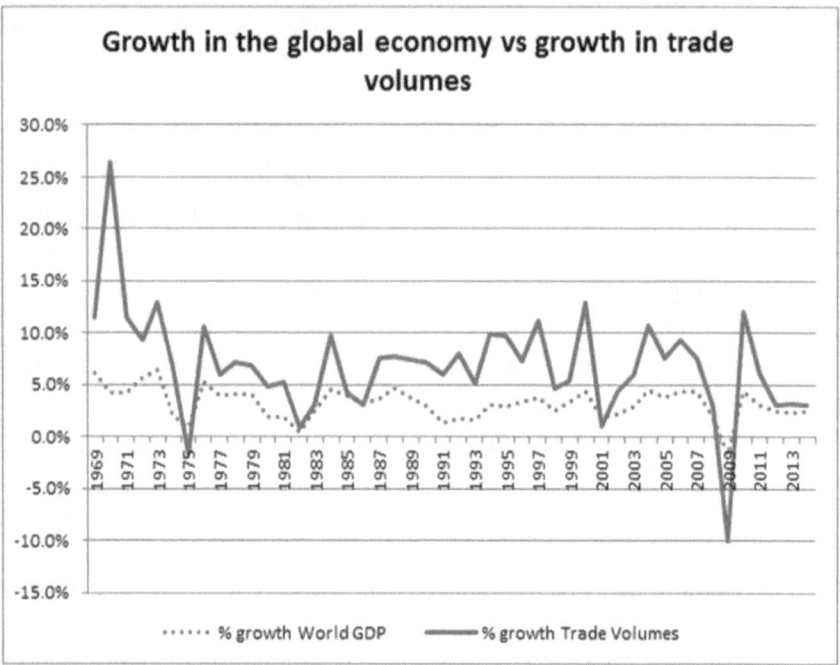

(Source: Author, elaboration of Bloomberg and international statistical data)

The Chinese communist system will continue to grow as long as we continue to feed it.

1

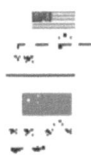 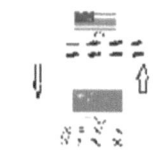 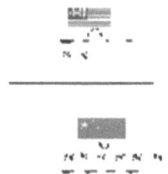

China destroys massive amounts of wealth Communist-style

2

China can only prevent its Communist system from collapsing by extracting wealth from other countries

3

And as our societies are weakened by this process, a full breakdown of this relationship, in which the Harley Davidson-size tick kills the host and then dies itself, similar to the process that toppled the Soviet Union, is not far away.

Sometimes in human history, things become so bleak that it is not just the adventurous that realize that continuing on this increasingly obvious path to ruin, instead of seeking a real alternative, is by far the most dangerous course of action.

In those times, even the normally conservative and cautious people, such as myself, can see the inevitable in front of their eyes. The real sign of "doomsday", if I may say so, is when those averse to change start jumping up from their sofas.

I would not even say the "inevitable need to change", as this would imply we have any choice on the matter. No, I would say the "inevitable outcome", which we can try to shape as best as we can to resemble something that is not too disruptive or dramatic. A Meiji Japan instead of a Russian Soviet revolution.

These are the times when even people who have a lot to lose and are otherwise very conservative, like landowner and slave owner George Washington, start to rise to the challenge.

The nuclear option is not to exclude communist China completely from the global trading system. The only really nuclear course of action is to keep them in, and continue to trade with them as normal.

And it is futile to expect that China will "reform itself" into a more pluralistic or capitalistic society. These Chinese Communist Party chiefs are incredibly risk-averse. They will do anything they can to make sure that they don't risk losing power. And they won't as long as they can make other countries' people pay for all the mistakes they have made, instead of just their own people.

Always remember that the entire shebang of "export-oriented Chinese communism" was an attempt to restore viability to their economic system so they would NOT have to make any changes to the basic power structure of the Chinese Communist Party system. When they saw the Soviet Union collapse, they became desperate.

They have not done all of this to change for the better. They have done this so they would not have to change at all.

Besides, the universal rule of change is that it does not happen if people generally feel that the current system is working fine for them. And for the Chinese Communists, this is still looking like it's working very well! Sure, they had a couple of relatively rough years recently, but compared to where they started, what they have achieved is still undeniable proof that the Chinese Communist Party is the guarantor of continued prosperity in the country. Think about how our side reacted to "victory"! Even we spent most of the 1990s and 2000s on a long and self-congratulatory victory lap over Communism, just to discover recently that they have been stealing our lunch all along...

Therefore, the only real solution to the problems currently affecting the global economy is to completely remove China from the global trading system, as was done with the Soviet Union. Without the continual flow of external surplus, the Chinese Communist Party system would not be sustainable. And we would be able to finally breathe free as well.

The global economy today unfortunately operates very similarly to a crime-ridden, gang-dominated poor neighbourhood. You have a dominant player with enough power to buy off or silence critics, and even though collectively the neighbourhood could take him on, in practice he will just continue to pick each person off as long as he is allowed to stay around. Compromise measures will not work. They will go around it. The only way to fix this is zero tolerance and hard rules.

Some people would advocate trying to fix the relationship with China by addressing their grievances on a topic by topic basis, in a friendly manner, instead of locking the country out of the global trading system altogether.

Well, we don't need to wonder if this will work or not. We KNOW it won't.

Why?

Because this is exactly how our governments have tried to address the problem of communist China over the past 20 years, and we know damn well that it has not worked for us.

Why has it failed? For the reasons we have already pointed out before. A communist system like China's is much more able to act in coordination with the different parts of the country than a capitalist government. So they will just keep doing what they have been doing. Cheating the system. Gaming the system. Guerrilla warfare. You bring an anti-dumping case here, they retreat here, advance there. This is a game that anyone who is playing with a communist country such as China will inevitably lose.

I recognize that only a large capitalist trading entity, such as the US or EU, is in a position to be able to take this decision unilaterally, given the size of their domestic market. But I can see this happening sooner rather than later. The only question is whether they do it just against China, or if things really blow up and they do it against everyone at some point, in a wave of unreasonable isolationism that destroys our good trade relationships together with the bad. I really hope it will be the first outcome but I am not sure.

Often in economics, the optimal long-term path has an immediate short-term cost, which discourages people from having to pay the short-term price to enjoy the long-term benefits. In this case, this would not apply.

Fortunately, considering the way in which the global trading system is currently set up, with communist China a part of it, we should expect an immediate short-term gain as well as long-term benefits from stopping trade with them. It has got this bad. By locking them out of the market for key commodities, we should see a major boost to the economies of developed countries, as well as most developing nations as well. What is standing between us and the optimal is not the short-term cost. It is a lot of other stuff. Like the pro-China lobby, including many Western businessmen, as well as most of the media establishment, complemented by this misrepresentation of "liberal" ideology that we talked about.

And don't believe those people who say it could be too complicated to implement this in practice. Nothing could be simpler! You lock one country out; the market adapts quickly! This is the job of entrepreneurs, not ours or the government's. A fresh breeze of capitalism! They will find someone else to buy from, some of them in our countries, some of them in other countries, and a lot of these jobs will be automated. It is a win-win for us.

World Trade Organization what? Everyone knows that any country of meaningful size can play with the WTO rules as they see fit. Communist China does that all the time, and that's why we are in this predicament in the first place! There is nothing either practically or legally binding in our relationship with communist China.

TAIL-CHASING - WHAT MANY ECONOMISTS SAY IS THE MAIN CAUSE (AND WHY THEY ARE WRONG)

In the next sections, I discuss the issue that, to me, can be almost as harmful as the impact of trade with communist China – namely the quixotic search for a "solution" that tries to avoid the unpleasant but inevitable task of facing the (red) elephant in the room.

Over the past 10 years since the most recent global financial crisis, people have looked everywhere to try to explain why things are obviously not working as they should.

Something on which we seem to have almost unanimous agreement.

Where people differ is on what is causing it.

I will avoid complicated statistical correlations, which in any case are often misleading and easily gamed to show what the author wants to show.

I will stay with the style of the true, common-sense economists such as Adam Smith and Joseph Schumpeter, who built their arguments on logical explanations from self-evident observations, just before economics deteriorated into an ideological trench warfare of people trying to save the world with unrealistic ideologies supported by often spurious statistical correlations.

Demographics – I guess developed countries only started ageing in 1995, and then very, very quickly...

When people have an ideological mental block against reality, they can seek answers in the craziest of places.

There is a relatively well-established trend, even among highly educated people, about seeing the change in demographics – i.e. the relative ageing and slowing natural growth rate of the population – as the main driver of the slowdown in the growth of developed economies over the past 20 years. In this view of the world, growth and general standards of living will not grow as fast as before because people are generally getting older, having fewer children, getting married later in life, and having to support more retired people from their tax payments.

There are so many ways in which this is wrong.

Now, as is widely known, over the course of mankind's history, the life expectancy of the average person has risen from 20 to 30 years of age to around 70 to 80 years now.

You may or may not have noticed that standards of living have NOT declined since the Stone Age!

Maybe 10,000 years ago, when you were in your mid-30s, you were old, exhausted and afflicted with a large number of serious conditions. Now we are not. We live longer. Because we live healthier. If we are healthier, we can work for many more years. And we accumulate more experience. And more education and training. This is not something that would be associated with a decline in standards of living, would it?

Because what these people like to forget is that the cause-effect often runs the other way around. When people are happier, richer, better off, they are naturally inclined to have more children and marry younger. Look around you. How many people do you know are delaying starting a family because of a lack of job security, having to live with their parents until they are 30, high housing costs, student debt, relatively low pay, or any of the conditions that have afflicted us more severely over the past 20 to 30 years?

Also, population growth is very far from a one-way trend. As you would expect, it goes up and down, mainly depending on how well people are generally doing. Consider this:

FIGURE 34 - HOW THE MEDIAN AGE OF SOCIETY CHANGED DURING THE 20TH CENTURY

Median Age: 1900 to 2000
(Years)

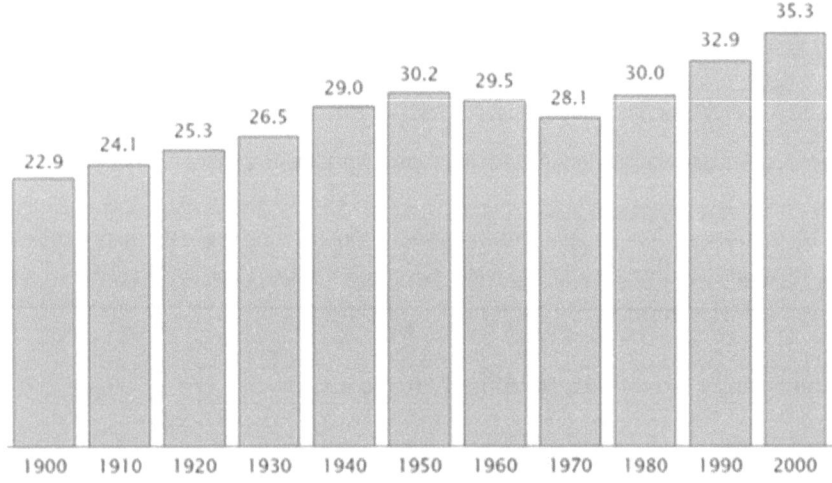

Source: U.S. Census Bureau, decennial census of population, 1900 to 2000.

(Source: Demographic Trends in the 20th Century, US Census)

When things are better, like in the post WW II years, people have more kids, the average age of the population decreases, and population growth increases.

FIGURE 35 - NUMBER OF CHILDREN PER WOMAN DURING THE LAST CENTURY

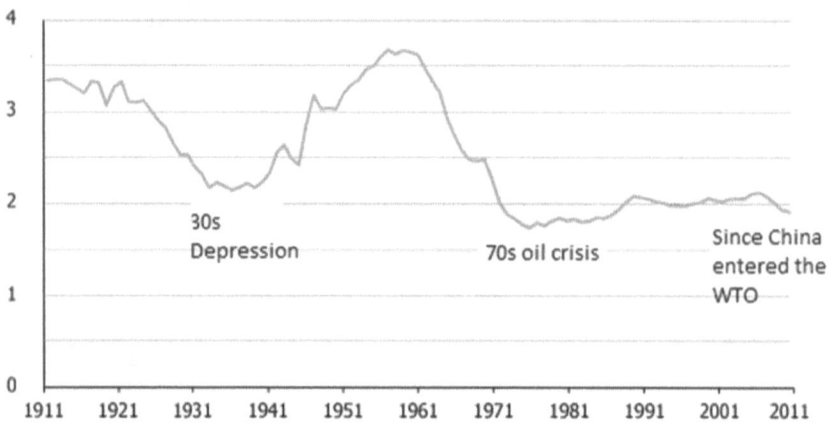

(Source: Author, elaboration of National Center for Health Statistics Public Use Data)

This is more or less as you would expect, considering that the heavy inflow of immigrants into the US slowed after the 1920s. Post-1929 crisis – bad. Post-WWII – good.

And taking a closer look, from the 1980s to now:

FIGURE 36- US FERTILITY RATE SINCE 1980

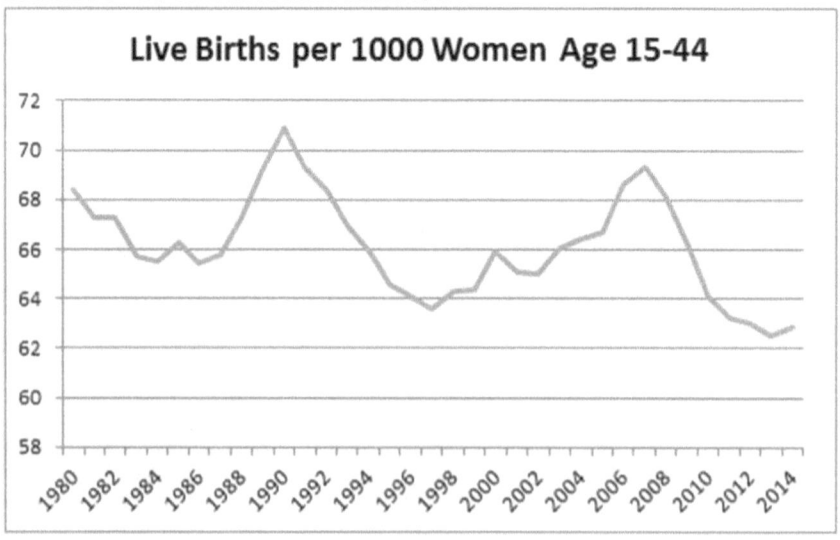

(Source: Author, elaboration of National Center for Health Statistics Public Use Data)

And consider how population growth has evolved over a longer period of time:

FIGURE 37 - POPULATION GROWTH SINCE THE INDUSTRIAL REVOLUTION

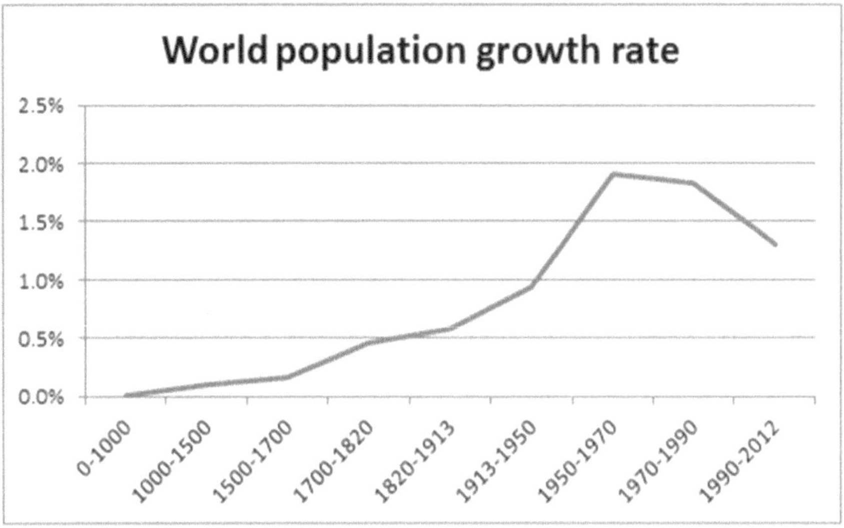

(Source: Author's aggregation of data from The Maddison-Project, http://www.ggdc. net/maddison/maddison-project/home.htm, 2013 version)

So, well, first of all, you can see that for most of the history of mankind, population growth was close to zero. This is because things were so rough that death rates, in all ages, were very high. Diseases, wars, famine, etc. The whole shebang.

So slow population growth has been the rule rather than the exception in our history. This is because our history has generally been rough.

During the period of history in which industrialization began to take off, our living standards began to significantly improve and we had to see fewer of our children die in front of us. So population growth rose. Remember, by the way, that the past 500 years is the period in which the relative scarcity of labour began to have the positive virtuous circle/chain reaction that we discussed in previous chapters – more mechanization, better production process technology, more productivity, more accumulation of wealth, better living standards. This is the period in which population growth rose as we started seeing fewer deaths in the family because of better living standards.

It is really hard for that to continue when heavily ideological trading policies suddenly throw 1 billion poor and desperate workers into your global trading system.

So good news! We will not "non-reproduce" ourselves to extinction! When things are bad we have fewer kids. When things are good we have more kids.

It is incredible how these otherwise smart people like to ignore the basic incentives that individuals have in an age of declining living standards and growing concern for everyone in this boat.

So these people, who will not admit to themselves or others that slower population growth is a consequence and not a cause of the hole we are in, will keep trying to push this argument.

For what you may ask?

To justify mass immigration?

Maybe, because in their crazy mind, people from poor and uneducated countries like having lots of children. Rich people don't have children. So if you bring a lot of people from poor countries they will "reproduce like rabbits" forever and we will have high population growth! No pension crisis. Everyone can retire at 50. Problem solved.

Never mind the obvious evidence that, as you would expect, as soon as immigrants arrive, them being people like everyone else, they see that the situation is not so easy and react exactly in the same manner as everyone else – by having smaller families.

Never mind that significant immigration is the major reason behind housing being more expensive, poor wages, and a whole list of other drivers of lower fertility. So it does not minimize the problem. Rather, it exacerbates the problem. And the only ones in the room that are surprised by this are the proponents of such a crazy theory.

So now you know. People will talk about "demographics" as the answer to all problems. It is not the answer to all problems. It is the consequence of all problems. If they want an excuse from ignoring the red elephant in the room, they should find something that is less self-evidently untrue. What more can I say?

Fiscal stimulus. Government spending. It only works if our problems are temporary. Otherwise we end up like the Soviet Union. And it did not work so well for them.

I will try not to dignify the stimulus argument with any charts or statistics. As it is so clearly wrong.

The basic principle of liberal economics and modern economics is that individuals, acting in a way to maximize their own wealth and welfare, do a better job on their own. I mean, relative to the alternative of having your government taxing everyone to the hilt and then spending it how they think will make everyone better off.

Capitalism versus communism.

So it surprises me that a lot of "liberal" economists see increased government spending as the way out of the crisis.

More government spending. More waste. As we saw, more waste equals less growth. Not more growth. Communism…

Taking this idea to the limit, you arrive at a communist state. Taxes are high. The government controls the economy. It didn't work well in the Soviet Union. Hell, it didn't even work well in Cold War Sweden.

So what are these people thinking?

They believe that our problem is temporary. When you have a very temporary problem with your economy, sometimes spending a bit more at the government level can make sense, they say. So people will not out-save each other into an economic depression where no one buys anything, or something like that.

That's where they are seriously wrong.

We don't have a temporary problem of lack of demand.

We have a permanent problem of the global trading system having evolved from a capitalist model (more efficient) to a hybrid capitalist-communist model dominated by communist China (seriously inefficient), as I explained before.

In the language of economists, it is not a demand-side problem. It is a supply-side problem.

Trust me, if we are not growing, it is not because we lack people or governments to go out there and overspend and then borrow themselves to the hilt. Just look around you. If it was just that, we would already be living in a golden age.

No, it's because we cannot AFFORD to spend that much more. It's because we live in an age of declining productivity, low wages, job insecurity, and all that comes with it.

And if we are in this situation, if your government decides to spend more money on stuff that people don't really need just for the sake of it, who are the only guys that benefit?

Yep. Communist China. No surprise that the benefits of the "coordinated global fiscal stimulus" of 2009 ended up all in one place.

So misrepresenting "liberal" economists defending the communist system once again... This is getting strangely familiar...

Monetary stimulus. Lower interest rates. Money printing. "Quantitative easing". Some benefits. But it is ultimately a form of trade war. Spreads pain to the honest trading countries instead of right back at communist China. Threatens the global economy.

Over the past few years, as things have remained bad, the false "liberal" economists did what they do best. They tried to find a solution to the problem repeatedly in the same old places, despite the obvious failure of these places to provide an effective answer.

They clearly don't take seriously the saying that the definition of insanity is "to try the same things over and over again and expect different results".

The people that don't like the idea of more government spending, with whom I kind of sympathize, decided that instead of lowering interest rates, they would print money ("quantitative easing").

Now, this policy was in many cases necessary to maintain the integrity of our banking system and national borders. In the US, the Eurozone and Japan, we would have had a serious breakdown of many of our basic institutions if the central banks hadn't done what they had to do. The Eurozone crisis of 2010–2012, in which the existence of the single currency was under serious threat by the reluctance of the European Central Bank to stop what amounted to a "bank run" dynamic against otherwise solvent banks and solvent national governments, shows that clearly.

The problem is that beyond the basic ability to avoid a collapse of the financial system, monetary stimulus is proving to be increasingly ineffective at restoring economic growth to a normal level.

Even with lower interest rates and easier borrowing conditions, both individuals and companies are staring at a bleak situation. In capitalism, everyone knows their own corner. The vast majority of corners are not looking good. Maybe you are a company barely hanging on. Or you have a decent salary but no interest in taking a risk and starting a company, considering how risky and weak the economy around you is.

Then you move to the main channel of the actual effectiveness of this policy – the depreciation of the exchange rate. It makes your country's products cheaper for foreigners to buy, and it makes their products more expensive here. More exports, less imports. It works well especially if you live in a country that has a lot of manufacturing, as in the short term manufacturing tends to be more sensitive and reactive to its cost structure than do its international competitors.

But as you can see, all this does is pass on your problems to someone else. One can only benefit at the expense of another. We are already getting to a point where the ability to pass the problem to someone else, even temporarily, is no longer working to stimulate growth, and is leading to conflicts in global trade. If we end up in a world like the 1930s, carved up by regional trade agreements that serve mainly as a wall rather than as a bridge to international trade, this is most likely the path that will lead to it.

Now, all of this would be fine if the only guys paying the bill for "beggar-thy neighbour" currency policies were in communist China. The problem is that this currency debasement policy effectively amounts to dumb, blunt, irrational trade aggression against everyone. Communist China is hit for sure. But so are our allies. Other developed countries. That threatens the kind of trade that is good – the type that led to the amazing economic recovery of the post-WW II period. In other words, it threatens the things that we should be trying to preserve.

And yet, in the absence of any coordinated political decision to stop trade, currency depreciation and devaluation is indeed the only unilateral tool of defence that capitalist countries have against the trade and currency manipulations of communist China. This is indeed why I suspect that we could be well on our way to the second-worst long-term scenario for the global economy: an all-against-all trade war. I say second worst because even this would be miles better than our current situation where the communist China fox has full and free access to the global trading coop.

I am not by any means recommending that the central banks stop quantitative easing. But I see it as just a stop-gap until the political consensus arises to actually solve the problem at its roots instead of continuing to play a dangerous game of whack-a-mole with the consequences.

Inequality. Serious problem. But like "demographics", more of a consequence than a cause of the hole we are in. Taxing Peter to pay Paul does not solve the problem, and can lead to internal conflict

A lot has been written about inequality recently, including, most famously, Thomas Piketty's book – "Capital in the Twenty-First Century".

It is indeed a major problem for our societies. The political, social and economic institutions of developed countries are heavily predicated on the existence of a large and dominant middle class, which is the group that has more to lose than the very poor, and yet more to gain from a functioning society than the very rich, who are not too worried because they are not really as dependent on the institutions of the state (police, education, healthcare).

However, this is where the consensus breaks down.

This is because many economists that choose to focus on inequality, including the misrepresenting "liberals", see a government-orchestrated redistribution of wealth, via increased taxation and social spending, as the best way to address this problem.

In other words, they are in favour of maintaining the current global trading system, but complemented by a small communist "thing" on the side, just so people don't fall too far and feel so bad, so they don't start questioning the massive damage that is being done to the trade channels on the external side.

Now I am very much in favour of the government trying to help people avoid extreme poverty. I believe this should be one of the main roles of government, and it is in any case how our nations have operated, successfully, for the past 70 years.

What I have a problem with is both the practicality and desirability of having this as a permanent solution for a large portion of our population.

First of all, let's talk about the practicality. OK, so you want to over-tax richer people? These are exactly the people that can pack all their bags and move their tax base to the Cayman Islands tomorrow. Also, these are the people that can afford expensive tax planners so they can avoid tax in every possible legal and illegal way. Do you think that governments are fast and efficient enough to be able to compete with their army of lobbyists and lawyers? This is pretty much like trading with communist China. We are likely to stay one step behind them at every turn.

So you want to over-tax corporations? These guys have even larger armies of accountants, lawyers and tax planners to throw against our lonely tax bureaucrats. Look at how much tax these large corporations have been avoiding already. Amazon, Starbucks, Apple…

Ok, so it is really hard to get the guys that are doing well in this otherwise bleak environment to pay what they should. Let's say we could make it work, for the sake of argument. Then we use all this tax income to vastly expand unemployment benefits and other social benefits.

Do we really want to live in a country where a major portion of the population feels useless and disenfranchised? And is, in turn, seen by the tax-paying population as something of a parasite? Would you like to be one of those people? Living on government handouts so communist China can continue its predatory trading practices?

Now, this approach would only work in two circumstances. One, if it is a temporary problem. As we are seeing, this is very far from the case. It has lasted for at least two decades. So we are on to the same flawed logic as the government spending folks – a "temporary solution" seeking to address a structural problem.

The second one would be if we were benefitting so much from trading with communist China that we had enough money for everyone to swim in it. So it would be worth protecting at all costs, even at the cost of turning a large portion of our population into "grown-up children".

This is clearly not the case either because the lion's share of any benefit from this trade is going straight to the Communist Party of China and its associates in the nominally "private" and public sectors. Trade with a communist system is also having the major side effects that we have previously discussed.

Keeping a large portion of our work force on long-term handouts does not solve our basic "supply side" problem of productivity and lack of technological innovation in the production process. Or the massive amount of internal value destruction that communist China needs to plug year after year with external surpluses. It is simply robbing Peter to pay Paul.

It is also important to remember that both inequality and attempts to eradicate it via tax redistribution policies have historically been a major cause of internal conflicts, including some extreme examples like the Spanish Civil War and the communist revolution in Russia. And that is without mentioning a lot of the civil wars in Africa and Latin America in recent decades.

If the price of labour is being debased, the solution is not to take these otherwise productive workers and turn them into frustrated people on handouts. The solution would be to change our economic policies into what economic policies are supposed to do, which is create sustainable economic conditions for continued improvement in real wages and living standards.

Trying to address the consequences without dealing with the elephant-sized problem that is staring at us is at best futile and at worst dangerous.

A lot of people would say that inequality is the inevitable consequence of a free-market system, and that the only way to fix it is to make the economy less free, in one way or another – taxes, more labour unions, etc. On this, I would encourage people to look at how median household incomes developed between 1945 and 1990 – a period in which the economy and the global trading system were, generally speaking, gradually liberalized. This is very different from the period from the mid-1990s to today when we saw continued liberalization but stagnant or declining living standards.

Capitalism itself is not a one-way road to inequality. However, our current version of "capitalism", which includes free trade with a large communist trading entity such as China, is. Our capitalist economic systems worked very well during 1945-1990 but haven't worked very well since. Capitalism itself is not to blame.

FIGURE 38 - INCOME INEQUALITY IN THE UNITED STATES, 1910-2010

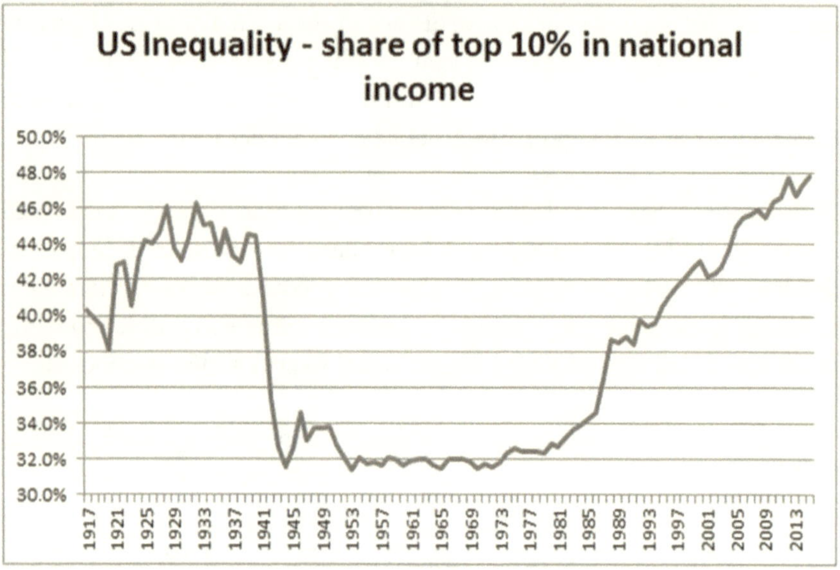

(Source: Author, elaboration of statistical data from Facundo Alvaredo, Anthony B. Atkinson, Thomas Piketty, Emmanuel Saez, and Gabriel Zucman. WID- The World Wealth and Income Database, http://www.wid.world/ 2016)

I generally find it important to highlight the significant rise in inequality in developed countries over the past 25-30 years. But I also find it "Darth Vader-like" disturbing that almost all economics authors tend to emphasize the issue of internal income redistribution and neglect the heavy impact of the current set up of the global trading system – capitalism in a communist bottle.

The most important driver of inequality, and the one that would be the easiest and least costly to address for developed countries – free trade with significantly poorer and in some cases Communist countries – has been neglected. This reflects the ideological mental block prevalent in the left wing, which until a few years ago used to monopolize the inequality subject, before even the right wing guys began to notice the social and economic ground rumbling beneath their feet and began to cast their nets wider in a panicked flurry.

So you have been warned. Be careful of "Lefties" using inequality as a banner. In their "global crusade for good", they care more about some poor kids in China than their neighbour next door who has lost his job.

Inequality exists not because capitalism is inherently evil. If anything is inherently evil, it's these people who believe that it is right for the population of developed countries to have a long period of wage stagnation as long as this allows some poorer countries to increase their standards of living.

And many of these people have a view of the world in which their lesser evil is justified by some kind of higher moral ground, and that they need to manipulate society one way or another into doing what is right. Don't forget that Soviet communism and the whole shebang was born in that same cradle. Don't fall into their trap.

Technology. It's a lot like demographics. It's blamed for everything. But its impact on standards of living is often misunderstood.

Technology is increasingly being blamed for the predicament in which we currently find ourselves. And on both sides.

There are those who say that over the past 20 years, the *rapid* development of certain technologies (internet, home computers, cell phones, online banking, online shopping, etc.) has led to significant destruction of mid-level jobs, contributing to the decline in the standards of living of the average person.

On the other side, there are those who say that instead, the problem with the evolution of technology is that it has been too *slow* in recent years. While our ancestors enjoyed major, ground-breaking technological leaps such as the mechanization of farming, the rise of modern water distribution systems, and the spread of the use of electricity both at home and at work, our society has seen technological evolutions that are much less significant by comparison.

I believe that both sides have something going for them. But ultimately, they both miss the point.

For those who are concerned about rapid technological evolution, let's remind ourselves of the same basic logical flaw of the demographics argument.

Over the past 10,000 years, technology has evolved significantly. We went from having to fetch water miles away to having it delivered immediately to our homes, for instance. Now, one man can do the same work of many, thanks to enhanced tools, working methods and machinery.

You may or may not have noticed, but standards of living have not declined during that period.

We should expect technological advancements to have a positive impact on standards of living, as indeed they have. They make products available that would otherwise not exist. They also make them affordable, by organizing the technology of production processes in a way that makes them cheaper. As in the case of "good" trade, they can cause certain disruptions here and there, for specific people and sectors that are negatively affected by them (bull whips, phone directories, paper manufacturing). But on the whole, they should have been good, not bad.

Now, I would generally agree that technological evolution hasn't been as ground-breaking as it was a century ago. But I think that this also misses the point.

First of all, some of the best periods for improvement of standards of living came during the 1945-1970 period. This was not necessarily a period of ground-breaking inventions. In many ways, this was a less ground-breaking period than 1970-1990. It was, in fact a period of relative technological stagnation. The 1945-1970 period had some changes here and there but nothing that compared to personal computers, cell phones, the internet, and videogames.

Between 1945 and 1990, it looks like the main thing we had going for us was instead capital accumulation and the significant rise in capital per worker.

Second is the bad habit of thinking of technological evolution as something random and arbitrary – a sudden spike of almost God-given brilliance – as opposed to what it is: much more boring, a consequence of the conditions of a society at a certain moment of history.

For instance, many of the world's most important technologies were first devised in China. Like papermaking. Or the compass. In that sense, China was way ahead of everyone else for a significant portion of the last 1,000 years.

Yet, when it came to adopting technology in a practical and widespread manner, the old dynasties of China fell way behind European societies. Think of long-range navigation, gunpowder, and ultimately the mechanization of manufacturing. China had the original idea, but for most of the time their society simply had little use for such technologies at the time.

As anyone familiar with modern technologies will tell you, those that originally devise a technology are rarely the ones that see it adapted to widespread commercial use. Home electronics were born in the US but only took off once Japanese companies managed to design and integrate them in a way that made them reliable and affordable. The graphic user interface of all modern personal computers was originally devised at Xerox, but because of certain company-specific barriers, it only came to be adopted by Apple and Microsoft. Kodak invented digital photography but it was Sony and others who were prepared to profit from it.

And so on.

Technology is not a God-given blessing of the random minds of brilliant loonies. Technological evolution and adoption are the products of conditions in a human organization and in society as a whole. This is because, in the real world, individuals and organizations respond to incentives. Incentives to work. Incentives to save. If there is no pay-off in adopting a technology, at least for the guys who are in charge of it, as in the case of the old Chinese dynasties or of Kodak, then not much technology gets adopted. Then it might as well not have been invented at all.

If, instead, you are having a shortage of workers because you are now selling to the entire world, like the old British Empire, the cradle of the Industrial Revolution, then you do adopt your technology. You use the compass to navigate around the world, and the steam engine and the power loom to multiply the productivity of your workers. If you have a big market but also an excess of abundant workers, as in the case of the old Chinese dynasties, you stagnate.

Which brings me to the heart of my argument on technology. We have indeed had many technological breakthroughs on the product side over the past 20 years (cell phones and then smartphones, Facebook, etc.). We even had some technological improvements that have had a certain impact on our productivity, though most of these can be traced back more to the 1980-2000 period more than in the years that followed - such as the internet, online retail and online banking.

However, the changed dynamics of the global trading system made sure that the positive impact of technologies flowed away from the middle classes of developed countries.

While in decades past, jobs destroyed by technology would normally be upgraded, now, because of the increasing competition with lower cost labour at the international level, the supply and demand balance of labour means that the main beneficiaries of this improvement are companies rather than individuals. Indeed, this is consistent with the economic history of the past 20 years, which saw a significant increase in the share of corporate profits as a proportion of the economy, relative to wages.

FIGURE 39 - US CORPORATE PROFITS AS A % OF THE ECONOMY (GDP)

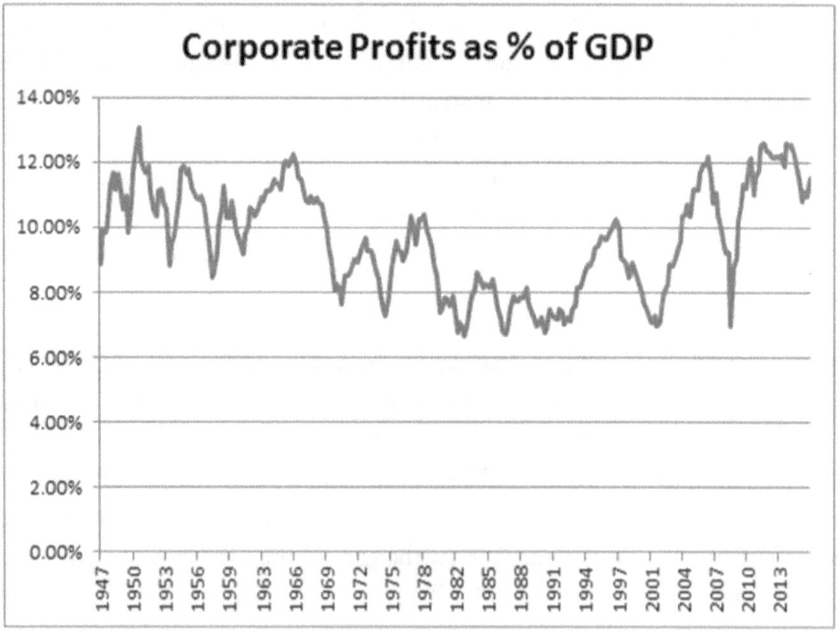

Corporate Profits as % of GDP

(Source: Author, elaboration of Bloomberg data)

Or, to put it another way, the improvement of labour productivity that resulted from improvements in technology did not filter down to workers, once again because of this massive change in the supply and demand balance of labour in developed countries. Consider this:

FIGURE 40 - CUMULATIVE GROWTH OF WORKER PRODUCTIVITY VERSUS MEDIAN HOURLY COMPENSATION IN THE US SINCE 1973

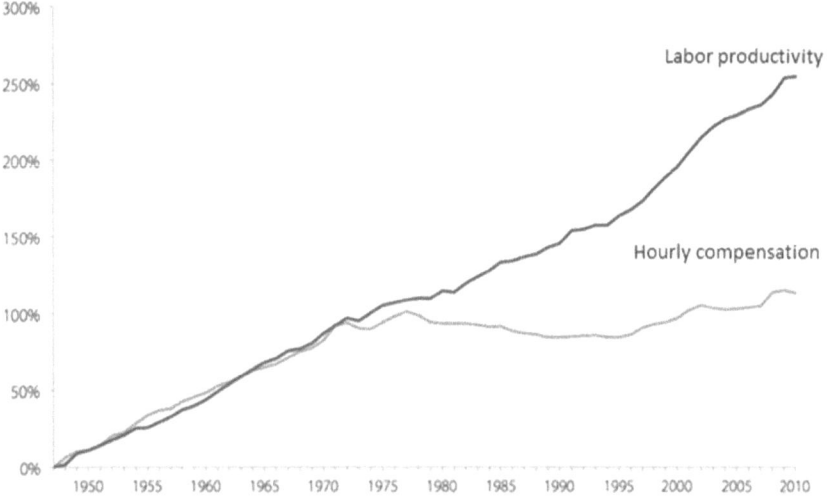

(Source: Author, elaboration of Bloomberg. US Dept of Labor data)

I would, however, agree that technological evolution seems to have slowed down over the past 15 years at least. Especially the technology of production processes.

But remember that in the real world, technology that is not profitable is not widely adopted, and in turn its evolution is slowed.

However, when communist China decided to re-join the rest of the world in the mid-1990s, there were suddenly more than 1 billion new cheap workers in the global trading system. We went from "British Empire" to "old China dynasty". Suddenly, workers were so cheap and globally abundant that labour saving technology no longer had the pay-off that it once had. Why invest in automation when you could just make much more money by transferring your production process to a low wage country?

Of course, the impact of the general abundance of workers in the global trading system, especially on the evolution of labour-saving technology, is something that we should have expected to have long-term consequences. And indeed this is what we are witnessing. But this is not something for our companies to solve. In a capitalist system, they are forced to seek the least costly strategy, even if these have negative, society-wide long-term consequences.

No. In a capitalist system this can only be fixed by the institutions that represent our society as a whole. Especially our national governments, who are still in charge of who they chose to trade with, and in which manner.

That they chose to do so in a manner that eroded the virtuous cycle of higher capital intensity per worker, technological evolution and capital accumulation is what has really impacted us.

We did not suddenly become less imaginative than before. We just removed the incentives to innovate and to adopt innovation, which, remember, involves a significant level of risk. And we created an economic system in which, maybe for the first time in history, the benefits of technological advancements are destined not to flow to the population of the developed countries.

Our ability to produce technological advancements did not change. What has changed is the ability of our societies to develop them. And to make them work for our populations.

Reforms. I am all for them. They are good for our economies. But they will be swept away in a wave of generalized anger unless we make sure that their benefits flow to our populations instead of to communist China.

In the economic press, even those that acknowledge that government policies such as monetary or fiscal stimulus are not the answer will usually float what they see as the real solution to the problems currently affecting our societies.

In this view of the world, all would be well if we concentrated on improving the way our societies work internally. That is, things such as more efficient labour markets, i.e. making sure that companies can hire and fire workers more easily when required. Or a more efficient legal system, so contracts can be enforced more quickly and at lower cost. Or the privatization of activities that the state tends to do poorly, mainly productive activities such as power generation and telecommunications.

Now, I am all for such reforms.

I believe that there is strong logical support for this view. Making it easier to do business is generally a sure-fire way to a better long-term future. It just makes capitalism work better. Sure, it may inflict pain on certain parts of society that somehow benefit from a less efficient economy – such as labour unions, lawyers, job-for-life civil servants, and so on – but this is generally more than offset by the improvement in the standards of living of the average person.

The problem here is that, once again, looking at our experience of the past 25 years, in which we have seen an accelerated pace of liberal "economic reforms", you could not say that liberal economic reforms have been meaningfully good for the standards of living in developed countries.

FIGURE 41 - REAL AVERAGE INCOME FOR THE BOTTOM 90% IN JAPAN, GERMANY, ITALY, UK, FRANCE, CANADA AND THE USA, 1950-2013

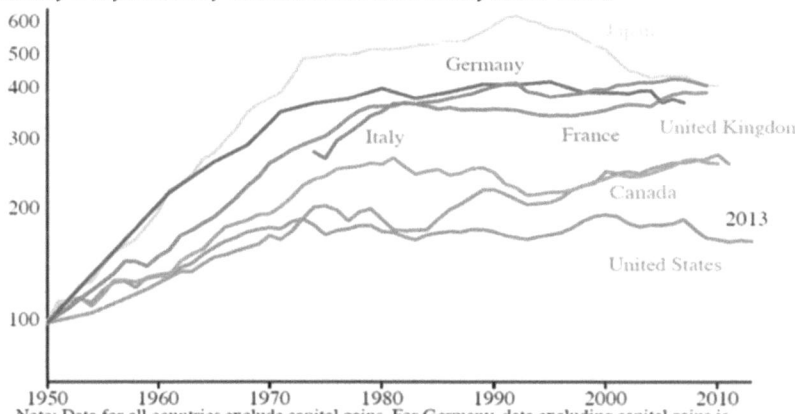

Note: Data for all countries exclude capital gains. For Germany, data excluding capital gains is unavailable after 1998, so this chart displays data including capital gains adjusted for the historical relationship between capital-inclusive and capital-exclusive incomes. Italian data begins in 1974 and is indexed to the average of the other series at that point. Italian data is calculated by CEA from the income level and share of the top 10 percent as provided by the World Top Incomes Database.
Source: World Top Incomes Database; Saez (2015); CEA calculations.

(Source: Council of Economic Advisers – 2015 Report to the President https://www.whitehouse.gov/administration/eop/cea/economic-report-of-the-President/2015)

And people around us know this. Oh, how they know this!

Here, there are two major issues with the "reform" camp. Firstly, as the majority of economists acknowledge, the positive impact of economic reforms is usually spread over a long period of time as opposed to being felt immediately. Secondly, once again acknowledged by most economists today, is the fact that the scale of the impact of such reforms is usually not large enough to offset other things that are much more important for the relative health of an economy, such as the price of a country's imports and exports ("terms of trade") and market access (think of Mexico inside the NAFTA versus Cuba outside it).

Consider this:

FIGURE 42 – INDEX OF REAL COMMODITY PRIECS

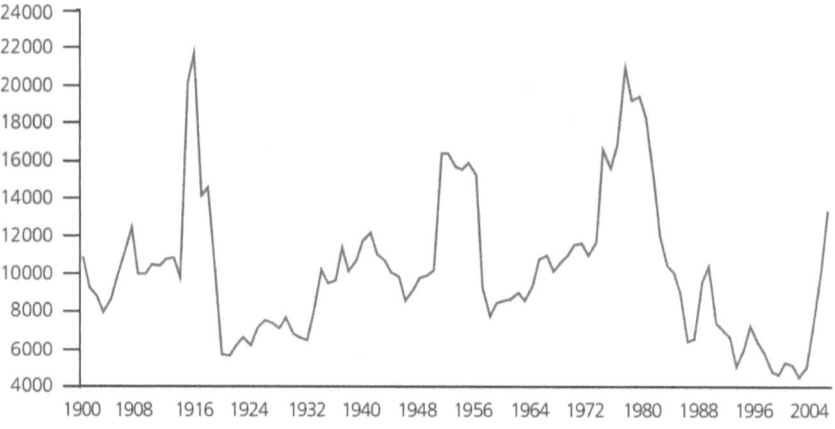

(Source: USGS)

And then look at how this has influenced a region that is heavily reliant on agricultural and mineral commodity exports – Latin America – compared to less commodity-dependent economies like the US.

FIGURE 43 - RELATIVE PERFORMANCE OF PPP-ADJUSTED PER CAPITA GDP OF
COMMODITY-DEPENDENT LATIN AMERICA VS THE US

(Source: Author, elaboration of Bloomberg and international statistical data)

Now, I am sure that there have been economic reforms here and there in many developing countries. But the key driver of a country's economy has been and always will be how that economy is positioned compared to others in terms of specialization, product concentration, geographic location, market access, and other factors.

So the impact of economic reforms is positive, but usually not so strong as to more than offset the key external factors mentioned above.

Also, remember that almost all economies in the world have gone through a significant period of liberalization over the past 25-30 years. France may have done less than, let's say, Spain, but both economies, like Germany, Italy, US, Japan, Israel, Canada, Mexico and India, have undergone major liberalization efforts nonetheless. State-owned telecommunications and utilities were privatized. Toll roads were privatized. It is much easier to hire and fire today than 30 years ago pretty much everywhere. Financial markets have been liberalized and internationalized. And so on.

Yet, as shown above, standards of living have stagnated in most developed economies during this period. Purely on a factual basis, you could forgive someone for saying that liberal economic reforms are actually bad for standards of living.

And so, you can see why a lot of people are saying that liberal economic reforms are indeed *bad* for the economy.

So you can try to make your economy better with reforms. And it will become marginally better.

But in a system where there is a significant amount of trade with communist China, which effectively operates as a monopoly on the global trading system, logic as well as economic models would dictate that a lot, if not all, of the benefit of this improvement will be captured by them.

So you can reform all you want. It will cause some disruptions in your society. It will lead to some long-term benefits. But most of the benefits will be captured by the global monopolists (Communist China) via the trade channel. Your population will not see things improving so much. They will question the wisdom of this course of action. Then there is a good chance that all of these liberal economic reforms, which are fundamentally and logically good for society as a whole, will be tossed away with the bad parts of our economic policies (trade with China) when they "come for you".

Once again, see how these false "liberals", by defending free trade with countries such as communist China, are effectively if inadvertently undermining the long-term survival of free market capitalism, and of liberal economic reforms themselves.

If we don't fix our relationship with communist China, we will not be able to reap the benefits of our reforms. Just like Old Soviet Communism, they will then be swept away, the good together with the bad, and we will be left with a much less reformed economy than before.

Reforms are great to have, but it will be increasingly difficult to maintain political support from populations who view certain sets of policies as failing.

ABOUT THIS BOOK AND MYSELF

I have spent many years studying finance and economics to postgraduate level. I have also worked in financial markets for several years, both in investment banks and in investment management. Over the course of my life and career, I have had the opportunity to live and work in many different cities, and in many different countries.

When you are on the front lines of today's financial markets, you have access to a dedicated news service, usually either Bloomberg or Reuters. This allows you to receive real-time news about relevant events as they happen.

Over the past few years, I have seen the world economy slowly descend into a fast-paced hell, and then a slow-motion train crash, on my screen, in real time. And I have seen the world's dominant policymakers fumbling around.

Unfortunately, when some ideologies become dominant, they have a way of both distorting sensible arguments for their own purposes and blinding otherwise very smart people to what is otherwise common sense, and to a certain extent, even obvious.

As I work in a sector that is very keen not to offend countries with significant economic power, such as communist China, I feel my career would be at risk if I were to be directly connected to this book. Finally, given the recent record of some of the most influential governments in the world - of abducting people they don't like in other countries - I would fear for my own personal safety.

The same reasoning also applies to most journalists today, including most financial journalists. Communist China is known to put pressure on professionals who want to speak their minds about what they are seeing in the world, both inside and outside of China. Say something against them and you can be blacklisted. The significant influence of communist China is increasingly being applied in the mainstream media to reward those that defend some sort of appeasement, and to isolate those that speak out against the current trading system as it is.

This is a game that an individual, on their own, cannot win.